Rural Transport and Country Planning

Rural Transport and Country Planning

edited by
ROY CRESSWELL

Senior Lecturer
Department of Town Planning
University of Wales Institute of Science and Technology

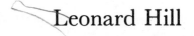 Leonard Hill

Proceedings of the Conference held at the University of Nottingham
in March 1977 organized in association with:
Royal Town Planning Institute
Chartered Institute of Transport
Institution of Municipal Engineers
Institution of Highway Engineers
Chartered Institute of Public Finance and Accountancy
by the Construction Industry Conference Centre Limited

Published by Leonard Hill
Bishopbriggs Glasgow, G64 2NZ
A member of the Blackie Group

© Construction Industry Conference Centre Limited 1978,
P.O. Box 31 Welwyn AL6 0XA, UK.

First published 1978.

ISBN 0 249 44156 X

Printed in Great Britain by
Robert MacLehose & Co. Ltd.
Printers to the University of Glasgow

The opinions expressed in this book are those of the authors and not necessarily those of the
editor, publisher or the Construction Industry Conference Centre Ltd.

CONTRIBUTORS

DONALD AWDAS, MSc, FCIT, AMBIM,
Chairman, Association of Transport Co-ordinating Officers;
Transport Manager, Devon County Council.

R. J. BALCOMBE, MA, PhD,
Public Transport Division, Transport and Road Research Laboratory.

JOHN F. BARROW, BA, DipTP, MRTPI,
County Planning Officer, Oxfordshire County Council.

ANDREW BLOWERS, BA, MLitt,
Chairman, Environmental Services Committee, Bedfordshire County
Council; Lecturer, Open University.

PROFESSOR G. E. CHERRY, BA, FRICS, FRTPI,
Vice-President, Royal Town Planning Institute;
Deputy Director, Centre for Urban and Regional Studies,
University of Birmingham.

D. W. GLASSBOROW, MA, FCIT
Director of Research and Strategic Planning, National Bus Company.

JOHN HORAM, MP,
Parliamentary Under-Secretary of State, Department of Transport.

K. R. HOUNSOME, IPFA,
County Treasurer, North Yorkshire County Council.

P. A. KEEN, BA, FCIT,
Chief Passenger Manager, British Railways Board.

V. A. KNIGHT, CEng, FICE, FIHE,
Director of Highways and Transportation, Cheshire County Council.

v

PREFACE

THERE HAS BEEN A MARKED DECLINE IN THE LEVEL OF PUBLIC PASSENGER TRANSPORT services in many rural areas in recent years, brought about largely by increased competition from the private motor-car. New approaches are now required to the provision of rural transport and to the related location of building development in rural areas.

Already in Britain, the County Structure Plans and the annual Transport Policies and Programmes (TPPs) are beginning to point the way to new solutions. Various experiments are also now being set up to provide for improved public transport in rural areas as a possible alternative to conventional bus services in certain circumstances.

Against this background the Rural Transport and Country Planning Conference brought together many of the disciplines concerned with rural public transport and its relationship with the formulation of policies for the planning and development of communities in the countryside.

The four parts of this book cover many aspects of the subject, from the broad social needs, through aspects of structure plans and the economics of rural transport operation to the new experiments which are now emerging.

In Part 1: Rural Development Policy and Public Transport, the needs of rural communities are considered, together with the place of public transport in structure plans covering rural areas. A case study of rural transport policy in the Netherlands presents a comparison with the British situation.

Part 2: Rural Transport Policy and Finance highlights the economic and future policy issues involved in providing rural passenger transport services.

Part 3: Public Transport Operation in Rural Areas examines the priorities for public transport in the Transport Policies and Programmes and considers the coordination of rural transport and the place of rural rail services.

Part 4: New Rural Transport Techniques deals with the various experiments which are being carried out or are proposed in order to attempt to develop new methods of providing rural transport, including the possibilities of smaller buses, part-time drivers, amended routing and timings, and the modification of the controlling legislation.

It is hoped that those concerned with rural transport and the related country planning policies will be stimulated by this book based on the conference to strive for new approaches to the problems involved, so that better rural services will emerge in order to help to maintain and improve the way of life in the countryside. The 1977 White Paper on Transport Policy (HMSO, 1977—Cmnd 6836) now gives greater encouragement for this to happen with a promised increase in financial support for rural buses and the possibilities of further rural transport experiments into the use of unconventional bus services and car-sharing arrangements.

Roy Cresswell
Cardiff

ORGANIZING COMMITTEE

R. W. Cresswell, BA, PhD, FRTPI, MCIT (Chairman)

D. G. Barrett, BA(Admin), IPFA (representing the Chartered Institute of Public Finance and Accountancy)

L. S. Higgins, MA, FCIT (representing the Chartered Institute of Transport)

T. J. Pasley, MSc, CEng, MICE, MIMunE, MIHE (representing the Institution of Municipal Engineers)

E. R. Pickworth, BSc, CEng, MICE, MIMunE, MIHE (representing the Institution of Highway Engineers)

L.W.A. Rendell, DipTP, DipTS, FRTPI, AMBIM (representing the Royal Town Planning Institute)

A. F. C. Sherratt, BSc, PhD, CEng, FIMechE, FCIBS, MInstR

ACKNOWLEDGEMENTS

The editor and organizing committee wish to thank all the people who participated in the arrangement and operation of the conference and in the production of these proceedings. A particular word of thanks is given to Jean Stephens, Carole Buckle and their colleagues at the Construction Industry Conference Centre for their efficiency in the organization and administration.

CONTENTS

x

FOREWORD

John Horam, MP
Parliamentary Under Secretary of State, Department of Transport

There are numerous complex interactions between transport in all its forms and the whole range of human activities: economic, social, educational and recreational. The Secretary of State and I and our Department aim to take full account of these interactions in all we do. You will doubtless recall that the formation of the new Department of Transport in September 1976 was greeted with groans by some sectors of opinion in the planning and environmental fields—perhaps some of you had misgivings. The new Department was seen as the re-emergence of the sinister band of 'highwaymen' which had been lurking resentfully in the Department of the Environment since the demise of the old Ministry of Transport in 1970. I can confirm that that particular conspiracy theory, like others of a similar nature, is completely groundless. This is not to say that the years of the combined Department of the Environment did nothing to consolidate and advance the trend to a more sophisticated and sensitive approach to transport planning on the part of central authorities. I am sure that immersion in the DOE was a salutary experience for central government transport planners, but this new approach was already evident in the 1960s, for example with the setting up of the Urban Roads Committee to look at the problem of reconciling much needed new roads with existing urban fabric.

Another product of this new more integrated approach, which came to fruition in the early 1970s, was the phasing out of specific transport grants to local authorities, and the inauguration of the system of Transport Policies and Programmes—backed up, in England and Wales, by Transport Supplementary Grant. This complemented the important statutory transport planning functions placed on the new county and regional councils by local government reorganization in 1974 and 1975. This major new emphasis on the role of local authorities in local transport goes to the heart of the topic with which this book is concerned.

We are concerned today with a special aspect of public policy for passenger transport, but it might be as well for me to state what I take to be the general objective of such policy. Put at its most simple, it must be to provide a reasonable degree of access to essential facilities for the whole community. I emphasize 'whole community'—in other words not only those adults with continuous access to a car, but people who rely for all, or most, or just some, of the time on public transport in one form or another. That includes many people—housewives, children, old people—in the 70% or so of rural households who now own cars.

The rationale for public transport does not, of course, rest simply on social arguments. In certain areas public transport can represent a better use of economic resources than low-occupancy private cars competing for limited road space, with the congestion that follows. The capital requirements for private transport in terms of road space and parking also need to be weighed in the balance. In broader economic terms, public transport is also vital for the movement of workers and thus has a key part to play in the industrial strategy. Nevertheless, in rural areas the resource and employment arguments are less telling than in urban areas. Generally speaking, the car user cannot be seen as the villain of the piece in rural and small-town areas, as the social rationale for public transport in the country is thus more dominant. It is true that growth in ownership and use of cars has been a major factor in the decline of rural bus patronage, but I am not one of those who regards travel by public transport as in some way morally superior to travel by any other means.

Rural public transport never has, and never can, match the convenience of an instantly available and infinitely flexible private form of transport. But not every family will own two or three cars! The teenager, the school child and the housewife need public transport as much as the working man or woman. We must make sure that the rural non-car-user is not left out by changes in patterns of housing, employment, education and medical facilities, shopping and entertainment which increasingly seem to assume universal car ownership. We should remember that universal car ownership is impossible. There will always be people who rely on public transport.

Rural public transport policy is clearly a part of, and needs to be considered with, more fundamental objectives for the countryside.

First and foremost among objectives for country planning I would put the safeguarding of agricultural land. It is too easy for people from an urban background, as most of us now are, to under-play the fundamental importance of home food production to this country. The British countryside—or large tracts of it—has for centuries been a machine for turning out food. This simple and stark reality is borne in on me very forcibly whenever I travel through the arable farmlands of central and eastern England (as I frequently have occasion to do, living in rural Northamptonshire).

But also enormously important for a largely urban nation I would put the countryside as a place for recreation and the objective of conserving its landscape and natural beauty and interest. That, of course, is why the post-war generation has designated national parks and areas of outstanding natural beauty; nature reserves and the like, with bodies such as the Countryside Commission and Nature Conservancy Council to advise on these matters. At a more local level we have the designation and safeguarding by county and district councils of areas of special landscape value, country parks, nature reserves, and others. Controls over development in these special types of areas will obviously be stricter, but everywhere the protection of the rural scene and habitat must have high priority in country planning.

At the same time in our country planning we must see that legitimate demands for building land are met and that the economic and social needs of rural communities are not overlooked.

But equally we should never forget that the countryside is a place where people live and work. Agriculture remains a basic economic activity in most rural areas, and is still a major employer in absolute terms. But planners must also be concerned with employment and job provision in other sectors of the economy and with the provision of housing, education, health and welfare services, community and recreational facilities and accessibility to shopping and entertainment facilities—which, of course, brings us back to transport.

A special objective of country planning arises in some of the remoter areas of the countryside. These are losing population—or at least their population is ageing—as the younger people leave in search of greater employment opportunities and better services and entertainment which the towns can offer. The basic cause underlying rural depopulation is increasing mechanization in agriculture, and the consequent decline in the need for labour. Successive governments have taken the view that an effort should be made to counteract rural depopulation and maintain a normal age structure and a health economy in country areas. It is here that the Development Commission is playing an increasing role in helping local authorities to tackle the problem by financing the construction of small factories, providing credit, advisory and training services and so helping to diversify employment opportunities.

There, then, as I see them, are the major objectives of country planning: promotion of agriculture; conservation of landscape and recreational amenity; and provision for the daily needs of country people both in areas where population is stable and—with even greater emphasis—in areas of rural depopulation. This last objective in practical terms means seeing that country people have decent housing, job opportunities, education and medical services, commercial and entertainment facilities, and the transport necessary to get them there. Sparsity of population and a scattered settlement pattern in rural areas inevitably tends to centralization of employment and facilities. This is increasingly true at a time when rising aspirations demand more sophisticated educational and other facilities; when modern business conditions demand economies of scale in industry and commerce; and when the wide availability of motorized transport makes centralization easier to contemplate in rural areas. I must say that I cannot find this centralizing trend wholly lamentable. How else would it be possible to provide really good modern medical facilities and secondary education for country areas; alternatives to agricultural employment—which as I have said, provides fewer and fewer job opportunities—for the rising generations of country people; a really wide choice of consumer goods; and some taste of the recreational facilities which townsfolk would not be without? Yet this modern trend towards centralization, made easier and more acceptable by the dramatic increase in car ownership and use since the war, increases the problems of accessibility for those without private transport, and may leave some people even worse off than more self-contained commuters of the pre-motor age.

This is the dilemma which rural public transport policy must seek to tackle. I have referred briefly to the new transport responsibilities of county councils, and—as the list of speakers at this conference demonstrates—those responsibilities place local authorities right at the meeting place of land use planning in all its aspects, and transport planning. As well as being the authority responsible for structure planning, the non-metropolitan county has, in the words of the Local Government Act, a 'duty ......to develop policies which will promote the provision of a coordinated and efficient system of public passenger transport to meet the needs of the county......' The nature and extent of those needs will differ from one part of the country to another. The number of households without a car, for example, varies considerably, especially between the South East and Northern planning regions. It can also vary between different parts of the same small area, as work on the Government rural transport experiments has shown. For example, in our Devon study area the percentage of households with no car ranges from 30% to 18% at different experimental sites; and in North Yorkshire the percentages range from 26% to 13% no-car households. The need to travel also varies between different age groups and according to the role the individual is playing within the household—the woman as worker, mother, shopper, engaged in leisure, visiting relatives, etc. In any given village, travel opportunities for people without access to a car will depend partly on how the accidents of history have worked in leaving a higher or lower level of transport service.

Local factors such at these make the quest for objective national criteria for determining an 'adequate' level of service a largely unreal one. The authority best placed to decide what is or is not an adequate level of service for a particular area is, in my view, the one marked down by Parliament for the job, in the Local Government Act—the county council. As a democratically elected authority, the county is equipped to make political decisions, and in a world where there is never enough money to go round, decisions on what priority and level of resources to devote to local public transport must often be political ones.

The central position of the county council in determining the present public transport needs of any given rural area, and the appropriate level of public funds to be allocated to meet those needs, is all the more apt when one considers how greatly the evolution of public transport needs can be influenced by the county's own decisions on the Structure Plan. The implementation of policies expressed through the Structure Plan and local plans will influence the location of major new housing and industrial development, and the evolution of existing centres of population, employment and commerce. In this way, the Structure Plan can over time have a profound effect on travel patterns and needs. Despite the difference in time scale it should be possible to relate the 5-year rolling programmes set out in the TPP to the components of the Structure Plan which will influence travel patterns. It does not need me to tell you that this calls for a thoroughly corporate approach inside the county's own organization, with the highways and transport people, the education people and the structure planners all conserting policies; it also calls for close liaison between the county and the housing and health authorities, and with the specialist agencies responsible for sponsoring and assisting industry and agriculture. This may seem a trite and obvious message, but I expect everyone can think of cases where liaison breaks down, even between different parts of a single authority, and it is a message that cannot be repeated too often.

The need for coordination argues for firm direction of local transport policy at county level; all the more so when every penny of subsidy to public transport has got to count and when lack of coordination at an appropriate level can lead to inefficiency and waste. I am all in favour of initiatives at the parish or village level in providing local transport services, but even the simplest community transport scheme should be related to a county level network if we are to build on and adapt present provision to ever-changing demand. We hear of too many cases where bus networks have failed to respond properly to changing demand patterns and still resemble closely the services of 30 years ago when everything else has moved on; here county and operators need to concert plans to make the best use of available resources. Equally, however, we cannot afford the instability which can result from the failure to plan comprehensively and from a reluctance to accept the statutory responsibility placed on local authorities.

Many public authorities and transport operators are taking up the challenge with commendable vigour. The National Bus Company have a continuous programme of operational development and have found imaginative and willing partners in a number of local authorities. Several county councils have been trying out methods of public transport provision which offer the prospect of better value for money than conventional buses in areas where demand is small in total, and geographically dispersed. One example is the use of school buses to carry fare-paying passengers—possible under a simple permit procedure since the Transport Act 1968, but still, in my view, capable of wider application. Another example is the post bus—a considerable success story in Scotland, but surprisingly thin on the ground elsewhere. Then there are the celebrated community buses in Norfolk, East Sussex, and Clwyd—the result of partnerships between the NBC, county councils and local people.

You will be learning from Mr Milefanti about the Government's own contribution to this effort to develop 'intermediate' rural transport methods, in the fourth part of the book. You will also have an assessment by Mr Glassborow of NBC of some existing experiments. The potential role of unconventional transport methods should clearly not be exaggerated. Their usefulness assumes that there are places where conventional buses no longer represent a sensible use of resources, but demand for an alternative to private transport is sufficient to justify some sort of organized response. I am interested and pleased to note that both the English county councils who are participating in the Government programme of experiments, Devon and North Yorkshire, are represented among the contributors, and I would like to take this opportunity of thanking those councils for their cooperation on that score.

Before concluding I would like to touch briefly on an area not so far covered—that is railways. I have said that rural passenger transport is predominantly road-based. I expect that even your British Rail contributor in Part Three would agree. However, he will point out some rural areas (including, incidentally, the area of Devon chosen for the Government experiments) where railways retain a place in the pattern of local public transport. These railway lines have a variety of functions. In many areas they provide an essential link with the rest of the country for business and social visits as well as for freight traffic. And in holiday areas a significant number of visitors may travel there by train. These longer journeys contribute important revenue to the railway network as a whole. These lines also fulfil a more local function for journeys to work, to schools, or for shopping. In winter they are regarded as the most reliable form of transport in some areas.

But rural railway lines are often relatively lightly used and heavily subsidized, despite efforts to contain operating costs. This was why our Transport Policy Consultation Document suggested that in some cases buses might provide a cheaper and satisfactory alternative, especially if they provided connections with the remaining railway network. Any alternative would need to have an assured future. This point has been stressed particularly in the responses which we have had to the Consultation Document. We are carefully considering all the views which we have received in preparing a White Paper.

PART ONE

Rural Development
Policy and Public Transport

Figure 1.1   Leyland National: the standard 'full-size' 52 seater single-decker bus used by subsidiaries of the National Bus Company throughout England and Wales (Western Welsh Omnibus Co. Ltd.)

Figure 1.2   Ford/Plaxton 45-seater, similar to many 'light weight' buses used by independent operators and some National Bus Company subsidiaries on rural services (Clwyd County Council)

Both these buses contrast in size with the 'mini' and 'midi' buses now being used in the various rural transport experiments (Figs. 10.1-10.4)

CHAPTER ONE

Mobility and the Countryside

Gerald Wibberley

As an area in which rural land uses are bound together by an infrastructure of individual houses, settlements, roads and many activities, the countryside has always been a place of isolation for certain individuals and groups. For most of man's time on earth people have had to live on or very close to the land from which they have gained their sustenance and their movement has been very circumscribed by the poor means of transport available to them which, at its fastest, has been the pace of the individual horse. This separation of individuals and small groups of people from each other could only be eased by the invention of a practical and cheap method of quick transport.

The development of the motor car in the 19th Century and the truck in the 20th Century, with the necessary road system, has greatly expanded the distance which people and their products have been able to move in any period of time. It has been reinforced by the development of quick communications such as the press, post, telephone, radio and television so that news, ideas and wishes can now be communicated across the countryside without the need for physical movement by individuals. There has been a linked development which has left people in the countryside with a greater reserve of physical and mental energy to use in travelling and in the reception of new ideas. The mechanization of many of their work processes, the development of the small stationary engine, the tractor and associated implements, the electric motor, better forms of lighting, heating and water supply—all these have helped to prevent the extent of physical exhaustion experienced at work in previous years.

These improvements have made the 20th Century a glorious period of time in terms of mobility generally in the countryside. People, the things they produce and the things they need, have been able to move so much more quickly and so much more easily than previously and have had more energy and the time in which to move. As with so many other developments this improved mobility has been patchy across the world, being greatest in the high income, westernized countries and at its lowest in most parts of the Third World. But the general message is clear. It is that the countryside in general has 'never had it so good' in relation to mobility as it has at the present time.

It is important to begin this chapter on a note of optimism and emphasize the marvellous inventions of the train, the bus and the car that have enabled rural people and their goods and services to move about more comfortably and quickly at lower cost than in the early centuries of walking or using oxen, buffalo, donkeys, mules or horses. The lower real costs are stressed because the walking person has always been expensive in terms of the wastage of his own energy and time and the use of the domestic animal for traction purposes has always been expensive in terms of the amount of land and human energy necessary to grow food which these work animals have had to have as fuel. For example, it is estimated that the horses used to worked the British agricultural industry before the advent of the tractor were consuming the produce of about three million acres in that each working horse needed roughly one acre of hay, one acre of grazing and one acre of cereals and beans in order to keep him going as a work animal. It is only of recent years that we have had to worry about the real cost of our new motive power, petrol, showing a tendency to rise. It had been falling in real terms in most countries since the end of the Second World War.

Privilege and Deprivation in the Countryside

At all times in human history there have been privileged individuals and groups in the countryside in terms of mobility and others who have been anchored. The contrast has probably always been much greater in rural areas than in the towns and cities where physical distances are much smaller and where public systems of transport were developed earlier. If, for example, one visits today the chateaux built and inhabited by the French aristocracy in the Loire Valley, the German castles erected on seemingly inaccessible and isolated hill peaks and the English country houses with their lavish space standards, it is obvious that their owners had enough private mobility to overcome any feelings of being isolated in their splendid living places. In contrast, most inhabitants of medieval villages and the small farmers of the hill districts of Europe were tied to relatively small areas all of their lives. Often this immobility was artificially increased by repressive legislation which tried to stop people leaving their home area and working and living elsewhere. Other isolated groups in the country-side were the early miners who had to live wherever the deposits of minerals occurred, and the scattering of people that accompanied the early developments in cotton and wool manufacture.

Though the general picture of mobility in the countryside has improved greatly in this century there is still a pattern of privilege and deprivation in relation to it. Today we could say that the privileged classes in relation to personal mobility are large farmers with their ample resources of cars and lorries and professional people with high incomes who can afford the two worlds of town and country through individual private cars and the use of rail and air services. The deprived groups are pensioners on small fixed incomes living in the countryside, children too young to have car driving licences, housewives left marooned at home by the husbands taking away the one and only car regularly to their daily work and all low-income people who are unable to afford a car. These groups constitute the rural 'transport poor' i.e. those who are denied the work and leisure facilities of their more prosperous neighbours.

But the concept of poverty or of deprivation is a difficult one. Should we be mainly concerned about absolute poverty or deprivation, that is, an absence of some or all of the necessities of life? Even this absolute situation is hard to identify and measure because of the shadowy distinction between absolute and conventional necessities.

Many would argue that it is relative deprivation which we are concerned with in this book, that is, those living in rural areas who, by reason of their physical immobility, are deprived and excluded from the possession and experience of goods and services considered to be the normal expectation of society at large. If the numbers of people in such a category are large or increasing or dominant in certain situations, then it is argued that state assistance to suitable public transport facilities should be provided. Some might say that changes in the provision of services in the countryside are bringing some deprived rural persons close to the absolute poverty limit, e.g. where the closing of a doctor's surgery savagely cuts down a person's ability to get quick medical help.

A third concept of poverty deals with the externalities of the problem, that is, the costs and inconveniences which are placed on the rest of society by the presence within it of a deprived group of persons. Modern society and Government are very vulnerable to contrasts of this nature and the media—newspapers, radio and television—are quick to expose them.

Judged by the amount of literature available on the subject of rural transport (1.1), the problem before us is one of relative deprivation of certain groups and individuals in rural society in relation to accessibility to goods and services accepted by modern society as being part of modern living standards. People who cannot afford private cars and are isolated through lack of a convenient bus service or one that is too expensive for them are deprived, especially if local services such as chemist shops, doctors' surgeries, village schools, general groceries and other services disappear from the smaller local settlements and are concentrated elsewhere. However, their lives may have been enriched in other ways. Facilities such as grid electricity, piped water, better housing especially in terms of sanitation, insulation and heating systems, radio and television, telephone, paved roads, access to a wide range of products and State systems of social security have all improved greatly for members of both urban and rural societies.

But why should we now want to help rural people when the whole history of the countryside shows that deprivation arising from lack of personal mobility is a constant feature of it? It is probably because there is an increasing social awareness that those members of the rural community who are trapped in isolated areas, owing to lack of transport, are generally from the lower income group and are therefore deprived in other ways as well. Improved transport facilities would increase the availability of all physical and social services.

A Temporary or a Permanent Problem?

Maybe we are even more confused because there appear to be two schools of thought about the nature of the problem. The first suggests that the problem is a transitory one, i.e. that with the passage of time all people in the countryside will be able to finance their own private mobility because of constant improvements in the motor car and other forms of personal transport. The second school of thought believes that the countryside will constantly reproduce its groups and individuals who are badly deprived in terms of mobility, and that unless we want to see a sharp contraction of the smaller and more isolated settlements into places occupied only by the mobile farmer, a few mobile farm workers, the richer retired and long distance professional persons and second home owners, some effort will have to be made to interfere with the pattern of economic transport services.

There could be a rather incomplete and unsatisfactory compromise between these two schools of thought. Already local authorities in this country have found that they cannot support the financial burden of trying to maintain a pattern of public transport services in their rural areas which existed at any recent point in time. There is obviously much change still to occur and the forces behind the concentration of public transport services and its removal from even more parts of the countryside are still in action. Any attempt to freeze them may be Canute-like and too expensive except for rich, urbanized local authorities with a relatively thickly populated countryside and a large number of inhabitants able to pay high rates on their properties.

Side-by-side with these attempts to slow down change there will have to be more dynamic action. A flexible but definite key settlement policy seems to be inescapable in most country districts but this need not be savage if it is accompanied by deliberate attempts to bring new local employment into rural areas generally. The problem of individuals and groups which are deprived of mobility relates back to the cessation of older forms of local rural employment and the creation of new employment in towns and cities only or at haphazard points in the countryside. Coordinated movement towards the encouragement of local entrepreneurs and the helping of new ones, which could follow from a more liberal approach by local planning authorities to their siting problems, would help to counteract the damaging effects of increasing disparity in access to public and private transport. In this regard the work of the Development Commission and its main agent, the Council for Small Industries in Rural Areas, in Britain, can be commended.

Interference with the market in the provision of public rural transport services by local authorities or specific Government agencies is both a delicate and a confused issue. The Department for the Environment is wise to go slowly with it. By the end of the book we may become clearer as to the way in which this interference can best be made on behalf of those rural inhabitants who are genuinely deprived in relation to their own mobility.

References

1.1 See for example:

RUNCIMAN, W.G., *Relative Deprivation and Social Justice*, Pelican, 1972;

RADFORD, G., *Rural Poverty*, unpublished M. Phil thesis, School of Environmental Studies, University College London, 1972;

Rural Transport in Crisis, Ramblers' Association, 1973

HALL, C., 'Rural Transport—A Poor Relation', *Built Environment Quarterly*, **1**, September 1975;

OXFORDSHIRE COUNTY PLANNING DEPARTMENT, *Transport Policy and Programme*, Oxford County Council, 1976;

ENMOR, P.D., *Public Transport in Rural Areas—a review*, Transport and Road Research Laboratory, 1975;

ST. JOHN THOMAS, D., *The Rural Transport Problem*, Routledge & Kegan Paul, 1963;

GILL, C. (ed), *The Countryman's Britain*, David & Charles, 1976;

HULL, A., *Mobility in the Countryside—A Case Study in East Kent*, unpublished M. Phil thesis, Wye College, University of London, 1977;

Rural Transport, (Reports on Symposium—4 volumes), Polytechnic of Central London, 1972-5;

MINISTRY OF TRANSPORT, *Rural Bus Services* (Report of the Jack Committee), HMSO, 1961.

CHAPTER TWO

Public Transport—A Key Issue in County Plan-making?

John F. Barrow

The Government's recent Transport Policy White Paper (March 1977) and supporting consultative documents are relevant to this chapter. Some of the proposals (e.g. greater decentralization and car sharing schemes) are reflected in this chapter. Other proposals (e.g. statutory county public transport plans and control of private parking) seem to imply greater intervention by local authorities. It is left to the reader to decide whether there are not contradictions in the White Paper proposals and whether the measures will slow down or halt the steady decline in conventional public transport.

County Plans

The 1971 Town and Country Planning Act, and the Structure Plan regulations, require only a limited amount of attention to transport, and that in general terms; on the other hand, if one were to follow the Development Plans Manual (2.1) one would be involved in lengthy series of surveys, alternative approaches and policies concerning various aspects of public transport and including modal split, provision for interchanges and so on. The more recent Circular 98/74 (2.2) however, comes more down to earth by making it clear that Structure Plans should contain nothing that is not of 'Structural' importance: the circular expects transport as a whole to be a key issue; it leaves it to Counties to decide individually what part public transport should play within their transport proposals. The Government's White Paper on transport policy (2.3) with its implied shift of resources from road building to public transport is one recent indicator of national policy thinking. The announcements on Transport Supplementary Grants show how these national policies are being implemented and include intimations, for instance, that fare levels must increase to provide some additional income at least to match the increase in costs—making it even more difficult for County Plans to show the resource implications of public transport policies.

Structure Plans

It is not appropriate to review every attitude which has been adopted towards public transport planning in every Structure Plan, but it is possible to identify five distinct approaches to rural passenger transport:

(i) Public transport should be maintained and improved as a means of reducing general traffic congestion.

(ii) A less specific attitude designed to minimize the transfer of passengers from public transport to private cars. This is usually accompanied by hopes, such as an intention to create the right physical and financial conditions for the most effective operation of public transport or simply to encourage more use of public transport.

(iii) Public transport is a socal service. This attitude is most often applied in rural areas where individual councils and examining panels have asserted that there is a social need which must be met.

(iv) The existence of public transport at a given level is a reason for the location of development in particular places.

(v) Where conventional public transport cannot continue without public subsidy, the answer may lie in the development of new approaches to the provision of transport, including unconventional forms.

It is proposed to review each of these approaches in turn, considering at the same time how far each approach could validly represent a key issue in Structure Planning terms.

An Alternative to Traffic Congestion

Whether public transport can be made an alternative to the private car to such an extent as to reduce traffic congestion is questionable. As far as country-wide and certainly rural transport systems are concerned it definitely cannot. It may have a chance of success in a town and its hinterland where political commitment to severe restraint of car use is allied to an acceptance of high public cost and even higher public tempers. Even with these circumstances a great risk of failure must exist, but without them, such policies are mere crying for the moon. Once a man has acquired his motor car at great cost, he enjoys its flexibility, convenience, comfort, and most of all its immediate and personal availability, and nothing but the most drastic action would prize him out of it. Setting aside

9

considerations of congestion, there are probably no circumstances in which public transport could be a real alternative to the motor car in rural areas, where the policy question comes down to what to do about those who do not have a car available.

Although there appears little prospect of success here except with the most severe controls in and near particular urban areas, the intention to introduce such controls would alone make public transport a key issue in any plan which referred to them. They would need to extend far beyond traffic restraint intentions to include financial commitment, public transport subsidies and wide-ranging and severe land use controls designed, for example, to protect the commercial viability of any town centres affected by a restraint of car use. Furthermore, even if this approach forms no part of a Structure Plan's proposal, it, or something akin to it, will almost certainly be raised by one of the conservation or transport lobbies at the Examination in Public. The superficial appeal of the idea makes it essential that any council is well aware of all its implications and potentialities.

Public Transport or Private Car?

A policy which seeks to minimise the transfer of passengers from public transport to private cars would appear to be meaningless, as it flies in the face of all forces which are leading to the decline of public transport. There are five of these major forces:

(i) A steady fall in demand for services over at least two decades, accelerating after the 1973/74 fuel crisis in spite of all sorts of palliatives.

(ii) The high wage element in public transport costs creates a tendency for inflation to push up these costs relative to private motoring. An increasingly higher subsidy is therefore called for to maintain a constant level of service, and keep fares to a level which will not increase the rate at which patronage is lost.

(iii) Little prospect of substantial additional public funds being devoted to public transport at the expense of other services.

(iv) In the absence of continually increasing subsidy the probability that operators will either raise fares at a rate greater than the general level of inflation, or seek economies within the services. The first of these options will accelerate the loss of patronage; the second will reduce the size of service.

(v) The likelihood that operators will seek to reduce the size of their operations; peak services which require vehicles to be maintained solely for that purpose will be withdrawn; eventually, a point will be reached where there are no net cost savings which can be made by further withdrawals, and deficits cannot be reduced. At this point, private companies will go into liquidation, and public operations will contract rapidly with public funds being used to write off outstanding deficits.

If you accept these probabilities (2.4) it is interesting to see how an authority might approach these problems in its Structure Plan. First, it might try to adjust living conditions for the day to day operations of public transport itself; in towns, bus lanes and other forms of bus priority, with some limitation on car parking, may help to stave off the decline of patronage. Such measures are not really open to rural transport. There, a County must seek to bolster up public transport by financial support if this policy is to have any effect, perhaps accompanied by attempts at rationalization of services. The outcome will be a rapid increase in the financial demands upon public authorities, and if a Council does not react to these demands for greater subsidy at first, it will eventually do so. Growth in public spending will not, I believe, be allowed to outstrip the growth in the economy again, and in order to maintain approximately the existing levels of bus service, extra funds would need to be found at the cost of another area of public expenditure. Would a Council ever be happy to see teachers' jobs lost, while they are paying increasing subsidy for a service for which there is declining demand? In Oxfordshire, the Council called the tune in mid 1975. The former County of Oxfordshire had been one of the first to pay a subsidy to bus operators in 1970. In 1974/75, the last year of the old specific grant system, the Council paid £216,000 in support of rural services, a sum which then was among the highest paid by non-metropolitan counties. By mid 1975, following large fluctuations in the operators' subsidy claims in the previous year, and with the public expenditure crisis building up, it became clear that a conventional approach of trying to maintain existing services broadly at a given level would not be adequate to sustain rural public transport for any length of time. Moreover, public dissatisfaction with the service was increasing in spite of the increasing subsidies, which thus did not appear to be giving value for money. The council decided to hold to its previous budget at £252 000, and no longer to meet the operators' increased demands.

Probably many other counties, faced with the outcome of a Rate Support Grant and Transport Supplementary Grant, the effect of their precepts, and a gradual but perceptible reduction in their available resources, will be obliged at first to limit their general subsidies and eventually to reduce them.

There must be pitfalls for any authority which includes a policy of seeking to minimize transfer from public to private transport in its Structure Plan based on an expectation for operators and public which the authorities are unlikely to be able to fulfil. Then, when the council is unable to continue meeting increasing subsidy demands into rural transport, what remains for its Structure Plan policy? In all probability, nothing.

Public Transport as a Social Service

Adding public transport itself (rather than the provision of mobility for the 'poor') to the existing range of social services is potentially extremely dangerous, and moreover it will not necessarily help to get the best possible transport service in rural areas. It will throw the burden of planning and provision onto an overburdened public sector which is cutting back on the services it now provides. The pitfalls of this have been described earlier. Nonetheless, there are some demands for transport, particularly in rural areas, which the local authorities may decide should be met. The issue which will be discussed later, is whether those demands are best met centrally or by some other method.

For example, how are needs or demands for transport in rural areas to be defined? Repeatedly on the radio reports are heard that this county or that is engaged in a massive survey of the needs for transport in its area. Can they place any real reliance on their surveys? There is a quite understandable tendency for people to express the want for a good which they would not use if it were available. Furthermore, among the immense morass of desires of mothers, children, aged and workers to travel for different purposes, it is difficult for the council ever to sort out which of these should be paid for out of the public purse. Some will suggest that this is where the Structure Plan should come in, laying down principles whereby travel purposes which can validly be subsidized can be sifted out from the rest. However, broad, countrywide principles for the allocation of financial resources to demands as local, complex and diverse as those for public transport would lead to particular local circumstances not being dealt with, those who do not need support being subsidized as well as those who do, and the country ultimately finding itself committed to far greater expenditure than it can afford. To meet people's requirements it is better to let them decide for themselves what they want within policy guidelines rather than introduce centrally prepared standards which will fail to satisfy some and appear wasteful to others. Such an approach should result in a greater degree of self-help within villages and will introduce transport that will help rural dwellers more than a short term bolstering up of existing transport services.

The whole concept of public transport as a social service is worrying. It seems another attempt to mummify rural life in villages, to deny the effect which the rapid change in communications had had on villages. It must be accepted that the *raison d'etre* for much of the country's rural settlement has changed dramatically since the war. Money cannot continually be poured into sustaining a form of life that has changed so much.

12

Public Transport as a Location Factor

Minimizing transfer from public to private transport may sometimes be attempted through land use policies as well as direct public transport support. For example, a council may decide to base its Structure Plan strategy on concentrating development along a public transport corridor, thereby trying to ensure that residents in the new housing have maximum opportunity to use public transport and that the transport along the route has maximim chance of viability. This is no help at all to the transport services in the large rural areas which are not on the corridor. Furthermore, while the increased patronage may help to keep a transport service alive during the period of growth, sooner or later that growth will slow down or stop; the public transport system will almost certainly decline, and a large development area may be left without the transport upon which it depends. There is a very great risk in preparing a land use strategy based on services which are eventually likely to decline or to call for ever increasing injections of public money to hold them together. Traditional public transport in rural areas will inevitably decline, and it is fallacious to base rural settlement policies on public transport services as they exist. Indeed it may be misleading to those who settle in the 'expanding' villages. Most families who move to rural areas do so because they have the convenience of a car for work and family journeys, but they may rely on the bus service which has been emphasized by the council as a development asset, for weekday shopping trips and the children's eventual work journeys. Some Structure Plans include a commitment to providing and maintaining public transport to these expanding villages, sometimes specifying that work and shopping trips will be provided for. This is a burden that cannot with any certainty be borne over a Structure Plan period. If particular villages are being expanded, let it be with the clear understanding that a particular level of public transport cannot be guaranteed, so that families who choose to live there do so in the full knowledge that they may in future encounter transport problems.

New Approaches to Transport

It has been mooted in this chapter that conventional forms of public transport in rural areas will gradually but perceptibly decline as public subvention reduces in the form of blanket subsidy from either central or local government or both. It cannot be proved that this will happen. Some observers have suggested more pessimistically that the decline will be so rapid that by the early 1980s our conventional stage carriage system will have completely disappeared. The signs are significant enough to pose both as real possibilities. The real question is not whether this process will occur, but how long will it take.

In either context the future for mobility of people living in rural areas of shire counties may lie not so much in preparing for unconventional forms of transport (although they will have a part to play) as in attempts at new and novel approaches to planning, and organization, embracing finance, management and operation; with even less importance attached to *plan-making*. The role of Structure Plans is and would be of very doubtful relevance or value. Plan-making in the sense of Structure Plan preparation involves procedures for submission and approval which are too lengthy and cumbersome to deal with the nuts and bolt of practical provision; and indeed the basis of that form of statutory planning is likely to be counter productive to actual requirements. Statutory planning carries the assumption that public transport can be planned as a centralised operation in which problems are revealed by survey, objectives are defined, standards set and services provided as an output of a process. Yet even with the most sophisticated survey techniques no centralized body can adequately define social needs for public transport nor find it possible to judge between them and then justify and be accountable for meeting (or not meeting) them. For example, is it more important to provide a bus for journeys to work or for a shopping trip to a local town? Who judges and on what criteria in a countywide context?

As suggested earlier, a process is needed which brings together the two major elements in rural transport—the user and the provider—in a constructive relationship based on the following principles:

    (i) Value for money in the eyes of local people
    (ii) Realism in its demands on public expenditure
    (iii) Some certainty that available funds are used to provide transport which the consumer wants and not what the established operators are willing to provide
    (iv) Sufficient flexibility to accommodate the expected decline in conventional public transport
    (v) Scope for innovation
    (vi) Recognition that conventional methods of coordinating public transport may exacerbate the rate of decline and that other methods of achieving the 'best' arrangement may not have that risk

In order to put such principles into operation an immediate and responsive organization is necessary: one in which the broad guidelines are set centrally (e.g. at County level) in terms of general policy and budgetary constraints; and linked with decentralized organizations (e.g. parishes, groups of parishes and town councils) where local people are in the best position to put forward solutions appropriate to local conditions and to judge which offer best value for the public money available. The respective role of such centralized and decentralized bodies could be as follows.

The role of the centralized organization (e.g. the county council) would be to

14

establish policy guidelines and budgetary levels, and also stimulate and encourage local interest and the establishment of local groups. It would hold discussions with bus operators to establish which services could operate without subsidy and would channel local group demands to the bus operators. The centralized organization would supply survey information to local groups together with advice on the problems and possibilities of unconventional services (car sharing, minibuses, voluntary schemes etc.), including guidance on insurance and licensing. Further advice would be given on the carrying out of local surveys and in the provision of publicity. The organization would explore the possibilities of staggering school and work hours, the integration of school and work transport, and their possible coupling with stage services, and also establish experiments with unconventional forms of transport.

The local (decentralized) organization, such as a parish or town council or group of parish councils, would establish the potential demand for transport and specify priorities for new, extended or altered services based on both a study of existing services and in the light of future demands. This local organization would be responsible for establishing local car sharing and minibus schemes. It would channel constructive criticism from bus users to the operators, and would prepare local publicity, including the provision of timetables.

Conclusions

By now it must be clear that public transport on its own is not a 'key issue' for county plan making. That is not because public transport is not important. It is. These conclusions question the relevance of the present Development Plan and its ability to deal effectively with public transport except in the rare cases discussed earlier where an authority is prepared to commit itself to private car restraint and major support for public transport including blanket subsidy. Such policies are, of course, a matter for the local politicians to decide, although the ultimate success of such policies is doubtful. Elsewhere, an approach is needed in which local communities decide how their transport requirements should be met in the expectation that conventional systems will eventually fail. The application of standards and the imposition of centrally derived solutions must be avoided; it is principally this that rules out any substantial contribution from Structure Plans. It will be valueless for examining panels and individual counties to fall for the temptation that a larger public transport system will solve problems of traffic congestion or meet the social needs of those living in rural areas; refusal to face the facts and to ignore the events of the last two decades could hasten the inevitable decline in stage carriage services. Planning must involve finding new solutions concerned with matters of organization and relationships; derived from political guidance and based on a philosophy of decentralizing decisions where they are responsive to local initiatives and

c

needs. Where such an approach is adopted it presents a challenge to planning (and planners) who will need themselves to experiment and innovate, unconstrained by conventional procedures and processes.

References

2.1 DEPARTMENT OF THE ENVIRONMENT, *Development Plans—A Manual on Form and Content*, HMSO, 1970

2.2 DEPARTMENT OF THE ENVIRONMENT, *Structure Plans, Circular 98/74*, HMSO, 1974

2.3 DEPARTMENT OF THE ENVIRONMENT, *Transport Policy* (White Paper) HMSO 1977

2.4 For a fuller description of the trends in public transport see WEBSTER, F.V., *Bus Travel in the Next Ten Years*, (Paper presented at Association of Public Passenger Transport), Transport and Road Research Laboratory, 1975; and ENNOR, P.D., *Public Transport in Rural Areas: A Review*, (Paper presented to TRRL Symposium on Unconventional Bus Services), Transport and Road Research Laboratory, 1976

CHAPTER THREE

Rural Transport Policy in the Netherlands

C.G. de Kogel

This chapter is concerned with public passenger transport in the Netherlands and in particular bus operation in the rural areas and the associated development policies.

The Netherlands is a densely populated country with an area of approximately 16 000 sq. miles (41 000 km²), of which 1160 sq. miles (3000 km²) are covered by water. The population is approximately 14 million with an average density of 1036 persons per sq. mile (400 per km²). 30% of the population live in towns and cities with populations of over 100 000. Nearly half the population are in the western part of the country, the so called 'Randstad' or ring city. The Randstad includes the metropolitan areas of Amsterdam (1 000 000 population), The Hague (700 000), Rotterdam (1 000 000) and Utrecht (500 000). The population density in these cities varies between 2600 and 6500 persons per sq. mile (1000 and 2500 per km²), with an average of 5200 per sq. mile (2000 per km²).

The Netherlands is a small country. The greatest distances from north to south and from east to west are 185 miles (300 km) and 93 miles (150 km) respectively. The relative smallness of the country influences the average distances travelled by passengers on public transport.

Governmental Organization

In the Netherlands there are three tiers of government. First, the central government seat in The Hague and often referred to as 'The Hague'. With special concern for public transport and planning are the Ministries of Traffic and Works, and of Housing and Physical Planning (3.1). Also located in The Hague is the National Licence Granting Committee, which issues licences to the regional bus companies. The influence of Central Government on public transport is predominant.

17

The second tier of administration is the Provincial Government. The Netherlands is divided into 11 'Provincial States' each with its own elected government. The Chairmen of the provincial states and of the Provincial Executive Councils are nominated by the Crown. The provinces have no direct influence on public transport and even their indirect influence is limited.

Finally, the third tier consists of the Municipalities, each with a Municipal Council and a Municipal Executive. There are over 800 municipalities in the Netherlands, but only nine of these (Amsterdam, Rotterdam, The Hague, Utrecht, Groningen, Nijmegen, Arnhem, Maastricht and Dordrecht) have their own public transport system. A further 40 municipalities have contracted with the regional bus undertakings to operate their local public transport. Although the influence of local government on public transport is strong, the influence of central government is growing.

In July 1975, the Ministry of Home Affairs published proposals to reorganize the provincial states and municipalities, by creating 24 provinces instead of the existing 11. The reason behind this was to decentralize a number of responsibilities at present concentrated in 'The Hague' and also to centralize some of the duties at present performed by the municipalities. With this reorganization, the problems of the establishment of a possible fourth tier of government between the existing provinces and the municipalities would be averted. One of the major proposals is that the new style provinces would be responsible for the provision of regional and local public passenger transport. At present there is strong opposition to these proposals particularly as the municipalities dislike the idea of handing over part of their authority to the new provinces. There is also great fear at central government level that the cost of this reorganization would be tremendous. Even if the existing objections were overcome, it would probably take a long time to implement such drastic changes.

Public Transport in the Netherlands

In the Netherlands public transport amounts to only about 10% of passenger travel compared with 90% by private car. In 1974 public transport accounted for some 8 700 000 000 passenger miles (14 000 000 000 km) of which 60% were by rail and the remaining 40% were by bus and tram (3.2).

Railways

The Netherlands Railways (NS) is the only railway system in the country and is owned by the state. Table 3.1 gives some data about the railways.

From this table two points are significant: the average journey distance per passenger is only 28 miles (45 km), and the central government provides nearly 50% of the revenue for rail passenger transport. This latter policy is based on Regulation 1191/69 of the European Economic Community (EEC).

TABLE 3.1   Netherlands Railways (NS) (1975)

Number of staff	27 000
Network miles	1740
″ km	2800
Passenger vehicles	2000
Passenger miles	5300 million
″ km	8500 million
Average journey per passenger (miles)	28
″ ″ ″ (km)	45
Passenger revenue total	Dfl.1150 million
from fares	Dfl. 600 million
from central government	Dfl. 550 million

Regional Bus Companies

The regional bus industry in the Netherlands consists of approximately 40 bus companies, which are separate undertakings. Some of these are private and others are owned by municipal, provincial and national authorities. The majority, however, are affiliated to the Netherlands Railways (NS). Table 3.2 gives some basic date on the regional bus companies.

TABLE 3.2   Regional bus companies in the Netherlands (1975)

Number of companies	40
Number of staff	12 000
Network miles	9320
″ miles	15 000
Buses	4000
Bus miles	155 million
″ km	250 million
Passenger miles	2000 million
″ km	3200 million
Average journey per passenger (miles)	8
″ ″ ″ (km)	13
Total revenue	Dfl.570 million
from fares	Dfl.300 million
from municipalities	Dfl. 35 million
from central government	Dfl.235 million

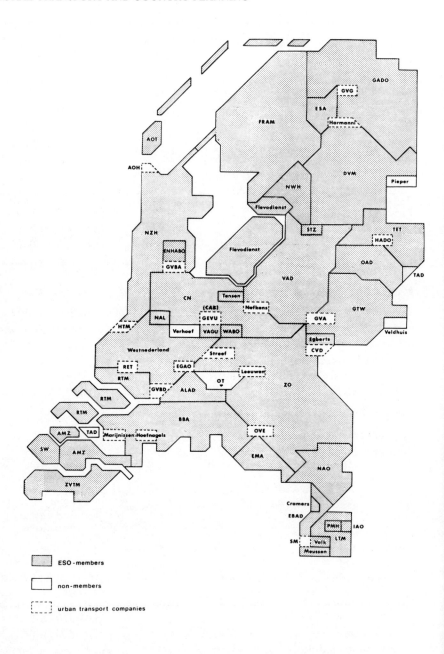

Figure 3.1 ESO joint management organization of regional bus operators in the Netherlands.

More than 45% of the revenue in 1975 for the bus industry was paid by government authorities of which nearly 90% was paid by 'The Hague'. In the Netherlands there are no other subsidies for the bus industry: no bus grants, no freedom from fuel taxes, etc. The average distance travelled by the regional bus passenger is about 8 miles (13 km); it varies between 5 and 11 miles (8 and 17 km) from one company to another.

Urban Passenger Transport Undertakings

As mentioned before, there are 9 municipal transport undertakings in the Netherlands. They all operate in the larger towns and cities. Until 1975 the Ministry of Home Affairs paid the greater part of the deficits of the municipal undertakings. Now an agreement has been made between the Ministers of Traffic and Works and the 9 municipalities so that since 1976, this Ministry has compensated all the deficits subject to certain conditions, the most important of which is that previous ministerial approval is required for the annual budget of the transport undertakings. Table 3.3 gives data on the municipal transport undertakings.

TABLE 3.3   Municipal transport in the Netherlands (1975)

Number of undertakings	9
Number of staff	10 000
Number of vehicles	2050
trams	650
buses	1400
Passenger miles	1250 million
km	2000
Average journey per passenger (miles)	2
(km)	3.5
Total revenue	Dfl.660 million
from fares	Dfl.190
from central government	Dfl.470

More than two-thirds of the revenue for the municipal transport operations in 1975 came from central government. The average journey length of each passenger was only 2 miles (3.5 km).

Cooperation in Public Transport

Since 1974 cooperation between the public passenger transport undertakings in the Netherlands has been growing fast. In June 1974 nearly all the existing regional bus companies joined ESO (Joint Management Organization of Regional Bus Operators in the Netherlands). ESO was created to stimulate a joint policy for the bus companies on every aspect of management. It also negotiates with central government about affairs of general interest to the bus industry. In January 1976 the nine public transport operating municipalities formed BOV (Policy Institute of Public Transport). The objectives of BOV are, to a large extent, the same as those of ESO.

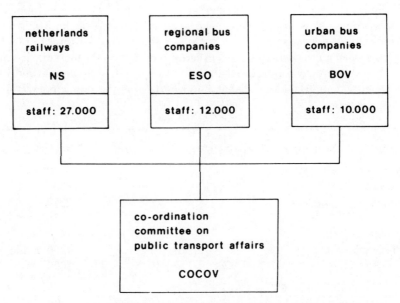

Figure 3.2   Cooperation in public transport in the Netherlands.

Rural Public Passenger Transport

Although the regional bus companies in the Netherlands have been working closely together in ESO, this organization is nothing more than a federation of 40 separate companies. Every month the 40 managers of the members of ESO meet to attempt to reach agreement on essential problems. However, the ESO structure does not make it possible to direct individual companies to give effect to decisions made by the ESO management teams. Nevertheless, cooperation is growing and the following two examples illustrate this development.

In December 1975, only 1½ years after its foundation, ESO published a plan for the development of bus transport throughout the Netherlands for 1976 and 1977 (3.3). This ESO masterplan not only contains for the first time in this country comprehensive data for all the bus companies, but it also gives information about the productivity of the industry (Table 3.4).

TABLE 3.4 Productivity figures of the Netherlands regional bus companies (1977)

% occupancy of seats	28
Number of staff per bus	3
Bus miles per staff member	16 000
″ km ″	26 000
Miles per bus	50 000
Km ″	80 000
Productive hours per bus	3130

The second example relates to the fares policy of the bus companies. In 1975 ESO decided on a general policy of fares standardization with an integration of fares systems. ESO aimed at a zonal fare system to be introduced by the end of 1977. In December, 1976, 60% of the industry had already introduced this system. Further progress could have been made if government regulations concerning prices policy had not slowed down its introduction.

It is expected that the tendency for closer co-operation between the regional bus companies will continue. In 1976 the Netherlands Railways, owner of 70% of the regional bus industry, made a proposal to the Minister of Traffic and Works to establish a separate holding company to encompass the regional bus companies belonging to the railways. The Minister has not yet made a decision on this proposal. Indeed it would be a far-reaching decision, because if approved, it is likely that, within a few years, more than 90% of the regional bus companies would then be under the control of such a holding company.

Government Policy towards Regional Bus Transport

Until 1969 inter-urban passenger transport by bus was a profitable business. The granting of licences and the making of decisions about the level of fares was guided by an economic yardstick. Since 1969 the deficit in public transport has been rising sharply. The regional bus companies together suffered a loss of 3 million Dutch guilders in 1969; this deficit rose to more than 300 million guilders in 1976. In the same period the attitude of the Netherlands' government towards transport problems has changed.

The main characteristic of government policy in the 1960's to transport was one of adapting itself to changes, especially to the growth of the number of motor cars. In that period measures were taken to match transport policies to the exigencies of a motor car loving population.

In recent years it has become clear that, in a country as densely populated as the Netherlands, this policy had to be changed. 'It was gradually realized that one could not go on with impunity making way everywhere for road traffic. The urban environment had begun to suffer; nature and countryside were being increasingly threatened', as the Minister of Traffic and Works has said.

By comparison, the number of motor vehicles per mile/km of road is the same in the Netherlands as it is in Great Britain (approximately 69 per mile (43 per km) in 1973). However, the density of road per sq. mile/km is 25% greater in the Netherlands than Great Britain.

The policy change mentioned above was presented by the government in a plan called 'Plans for Better Traffic Management' (3.4) (the so called Multi-Year Plan for Passenger Transport (MPP)) covering the period 1976-1980, published in November 1975. The plan contained the following goals:

    (i) Slowing down of mobility growth
    (ii) Restriction of motor traffic, especially in conurbations
    (iii) Promotion of the use of public transport

A variety of measures described in the five year plan will be developed to reach the above mentioned goals. The basic principles concerning public passenger transport are summarized as follows:

    (i) The level of provision of public transport will remain roughly as at present and fares will be kept in step with the cost of living.
    (ii) Traffic priority measures will increase the capacity of urban and regional public transport.
    (iii) The efficiency of public transport will be increased as much as possible.

An interesting point in the context of this Chapter is that very little is said in the five-year plan about transport in rural areas, where the space problem is not yet urgent. However, it states that the plan does not intend to restrict car use in the countryside.

One of the most serious problems nowadays in realizing government policy is the budget problem. There is simply not enough money to realize all the proposals. Given the fact that one quarter of the budget of the Ministry of Traffic and Works is needed to cover the deficits of public transport (rail, local and regional bus companies together), there is obviously little additional capital available. Public transport in general must not exceed the amounts in the ministerial budget.

Standardization of Service Level

In the Netherlands, the licensing of regional public passenger transport together with the setting of service level standards, such as frequencies, is to a great extent centralized. Nevertheless, within the 40 separate bus companies, there is still a large variety of service levels throughout the country. The principal reason for this is the influence of the Regional Inspectors of Traffic, who have their own responsibility to approve service frequency proposals from the bus companies. These variations occur although the Regional Inspectors of Traffic are civil servants of the Ministry of Traffic and Works.

One of the means chosen by the Minister of Traffic and Works to control the rise in the deficits of the regional bus companies is the standardization of service levels. In 1976, the Ministry started, in close cooperation with ESO, the development of such a system. It was based on a certain ratio between the offered bus capacity and the actual demand per hour and per section of a route, together with the following four points which are taken into account:

    (i) An operating aspect: circulation of buses and staff.
    (ii) A marketing aspect: regularity in the time table.
    (iii) An integration aspect: relationship with rail and local buses.
    (iv) A social aspect: minimum frequency.

The system will be in operation by the first half of 1979. In order to maintain equilibrium between the service levels of the different public passenger transport systems, it was intended that similar standardization methods should be employed by local passenger transport undertakings. The Netherlands Railways are also practising a similar system.

Environment and Rural Transport

Generally speaking, there is in the Netherlands a highly-developed public passenger transport system compared with many other countries. This is also true for the rural areas. The main reasons for this are, of course, the density of population and the relatively short distances involved in the Netherlands.

The formation of the regional bus companies over the years has prevented an unbalanced development of public transport. Until now there have been hardly any 'white areas' on the public transport map of the Netherlands. The view that traffic and transport are essential elements in physical planning is growing at all levels of the planning process.

The three tiers of government in the Netherlands have already been described. The role of each of the three levels in relation to physical planning is now considered, with special reference to rural transport.

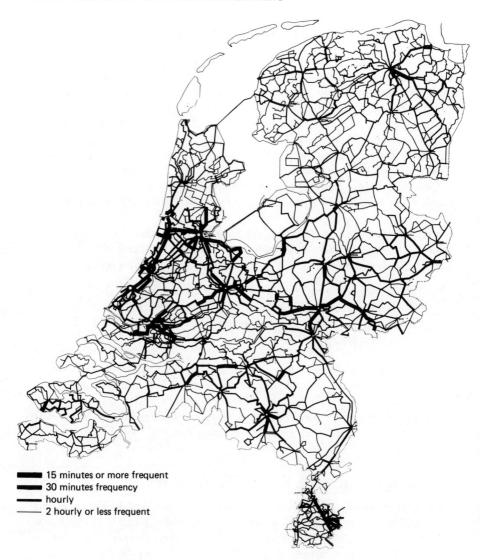

━━━ 15 minutes or more frequent
━━ 30 minutes frequency
━ hourly
─── 2 hourly or less frequent

Figure 3.3   Bus routes in the Netherlands

Central Government

The Ministry of Housing and Physical Planning, responsible for coordinated land-use planning, is now developing the 'Third Report on Physical Planning'. This plan is being built up step by step and a draft Nationwide Policy for the Development of Towns was published in 1976. In 1977 a draft policy for countryside planning was due to follow.

26

PHYSICAL PLANNING ACT

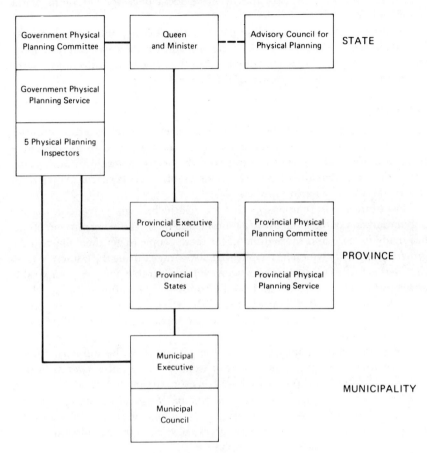

Figure 3.4   Physical Planning Act in the Netherlands

In March 1977, a Structure Traffic and Transport Scheme was published under the authority of the Minister of Traffic and Works. This Scheme is a plan in which the needs of the transport and the possibilities for the environment are weighed one against the other. At least 10 of these schemes on different subjects will be published in due course. All these plans cover a long-term period (25-30 years ahead) and are subject to widespread consultation with the public.

Provinces

The provincial councils play an important role in physical planning. They are responsible for the development of regional plans and each province has a Physical Planning Committee and a Physical Planning Department. The

Provincial Government also approves the local development plans of the municipalities.

The growing interest of the Provincial Authorities in public transport as an important element in physical planning, including rural areas, can be demonstrated by the following two examples from the provinces of Groningen in the north and Utrecht in the centre of the Netherlands.

Groningen

The Provincial Executive Council of Groningen in 1975 established a committee charged with the task of developing a provincial policy plan for passenger traffic and transport. The committee with the help of several working parties has made a thorough investigation of all the problems concerned and their draft report has already been published (3.5).

This draft report emphasises that a relatively high percentage of the population do not have the use of a motor car. The fast-growing number of cars has made it more and more difficult for these people to get their share in the growth of mobility which has triplicated on average during the last ten years in the Netherlands. Circumstances were not favourable for the comparable development of the bicycle and public transport. The number of bicycles is estimated to be some 8 million, of which 70% are regularly used. The committee felt that any further restriction in the development of both modes of transport should be avoided.

The report gives details of the traffic problems in the infrastructure of Groningen and on the quality of the existing public passenger transport services. The future proposals are based on estimates made by realistic growth models in which population increase, regional physical planning, mobility growth etc. each play a role. The social aspects influencing the mobility growth; schools, shopping, contact with relatives, participation in cultural events, recreation, etc. are particularly emphasized.

The systematic evaluation of the public passenger transport system at present and in the near future concerns:

(i) The frequency of the service offered to and from the nearest large town and to and from the regional centre of Groningen (the capital of the Province of Groningen).
(ii) The number of passenger journeys per day.
(iii) The time between first and last journey.
(iv) The accessibility of the national rail system.
(v) The average speed of journey (including changing times).

Furthermore, the study outlines the possibilities of reorganization and recommends several changes in service level on the public passenger transport system. However, the financial problems are paramount. The provinces have

28

only limited resources of income, mainly coming from the state. There are no separate funds for financing public transport as there are, for example, for road building. One of the conclusions of the committee is, that in balancing the cost and effects of investment in road building, or in the requirements of public transport, cyclists and pedestrians, the last mentioned category should be favoured. However, until now it has not been possible for the provincial council to subsidize public passenger transport. On the contrary, as mentioned before, the Ministry of Traffic and Works has recently taken measures to the effect that all the deficits of public passenger transport would be covered via this Ministry, while plans to develop urban and regional public transport must be approved by the Ministry.

Utrecht

In 1973 the Province of Utrecht published a report 'Regional Public Transport in the Province of Utrecht'. In this study a simple and pragmatic method is developed to judge the service levels of regional public transport. The factors taken into account were: the population of the settlements, the distance to the regional centre, the proximity of railway stations and bus routes, and the frequencies of the public transport services. A thorough comparison of all existing services in the province resulted in proposals for a preferential service level, which are summarized in Table 3.5.

TABLE 3.5   Outline of preferential service levels of public passenger transport—Province of Utrecht

Number of inhabitants of a population cluster	Distance to a service area			
	5–10 km	10–15 km	15–20 km	more than 20 km
1000 – 4000	30 min	60 min	60 min	60 min
4000 – 6000	15 min	30 min	60 min	60 min
6000 – 8000	15 min	15 min	30 min	60 min
8000 – 10 000	15 min	15 min	30 min	30 min
10 000 – 15 000	10 min	15 min	15 min	30 min
15 000 – 20 000	5–10 min	10 min	15 min	15 min
20 000 – 30 000	5 min	5–10 min	10 min	15 min
more than 30 000	5 min	5 min	5–10 min	10 min

Application of the scheme to the existing situation in the province of Utrecht leads to proposals for the improvement of both service frequencies and routes. Here again, the implementation of the recommendations depends on the availability of financial resources from central government. Nevertheless, ESO

29

is very pleased with this growing interest in public transport policy at the provincial level.

Municipalities

Each municipality is required to prepare a physical development plan for its territory. Increasingly, it is felt that such a plan should pay special attention to traffic problems in general and to public passenger transport in particular.

In order to get financial assistance from the Central Government to undertake improvements, each municipality has to prepare short-term traffic and transportation plans.

The smaller rural municipalities with few or no traffic problems are generally ill-equipped for playing a significant role in the transportation aspects of physical planning. Nevertheless, it is important for the regional bus companies to have good relationships with the municipalities in order to participate in the preparation of local development plans.

Conclusion

It will be seen from this Chapter that public passenger transport is receiving increasing attention from the three tiers of government in the Netherlands and is becoming a greater part of the overall physical planning policy, in rural as well as urban areas.

References

3.1 BOMMER, T., *Housing and Planning Legislation in the Netherlands Bonncentrum*, Rotterdam, 1967
3.2 CENTRAL BUREAU OF STATISTICS OF THE NETHERLANDS, *Statistical Yearbook 1975*
3.3 ESO, *Bedrijfstakplan 1977*, Planbureau ESO, Utrecht, December 1975; and *Streekvervoer 1975*, Annual Report, Utrecht, July 1976
3.4 MINISTRY OF TRAFFIC AND WORKS, *Plans for Better Traffic Management*, (Summary of a Multi-Year Plan for Passenger Transport 1976-80), Information Department, The Hague, 1976
3.5 PROVINCIE GRONINGEN, Interim rapportage *Belerdsnota Personen Verkeer en Vervoer*, Groningen 75-11-20 en 76-05-03

PART ONE DISCUSSION
Rural Development Policy and
Public Transport
Chairman: Gordon Cherry

P.M.D. LUTMAN (City of Oxford Motor Services Ltd),

Mr. Barrow may have given the impression that Oxford Motor Services receive approximately 96% of their revenue in support grants and 4% in fares. In reality, though, even at the maximum level of support the reverse was the case and currently it receives no revenue support grant at all.

Financial estimates referred to by Mr. Barrow were made at different times on different bases in a period of 28% inflation both before and after fares applications had been heard and granted; so there is inevitably a wide fluctuation in the requests for or anticipated amounts of revenue support needed.

Thirdly, regarding the figure of 75 passengers per day enjoying travel facilities for a £300 000 subsidy (i.e. 45 000 passengers per annum), we estimate that at least half a million passengers per annum were affected by the changes in services provided. So far, 16 buses have been withdrawn and traffic commissioners' approval to withdraw a further three is awaited; the withdrawal has been delayed by county council objections to the licence applications. Withdrawing a bus at 7.45 a.m. to town A and leaving a bus at 11.00 a.m. to town B may seem a reasonable alternative to the county council but it is doubtful if the passengers would agree.

Parish groups are supported by the company; anything that facilitates contact with customers must be beneficial, but only within certain limits. There are real dangers of the county devolving its coordination role to parish groups. The groups are there to be selfish, to pursue their local needs without regard to the needs of other groups, other districts or indeed other counties. It is necessary to look a little wider than parish groups in the context of coordination.

DR. A. OCHOJNA (Greater Glasgow Passenger Transport Executive)

Greater Glasgow PTE has the transport planning function for the Strathclyde region which covers 4000 sq. miles (10 360 km²) of rural land containing a population of a third of a million. A rural public transport policy study has been completed and one of the major problems has been deciding the size of subsidy

D

31

that should be allocated to rural areas. It is important, when looking at rural areas, to decide how much they contribute to the region or the county. Strathclyde Regional Council realize that the rural population plays a very vital part in the community and therefore should be looked at in the same light as the urban population when subsidies are allocated.

It is important to realize how difficult it is to set up minimum levels of service. It would be almost impossible to define the minimum level of service and, accepting that there is a valid rural population (i.e. one to provide labour for primary industries), there appears no reason why it should be submitted to some kind of transport means test while millions of pounds are pumped into moving the urban workers around. In a region which has both a vast urban and a vast rural area there are difficulties in splitting the resources between the areas. If the rural area is studied in isolation and too great an emphasis is placed on minimum levels, this vital point may be missed.

P. DEAVIN (Norfolk County Council)

Millions of pounds should not be put into buses in conurbations by subsidizing fares when the same cannot be afforded in the rural areas.

What does Mr. Barrow consider rural transport need to be? Little sympathy can be given to the wealthy person who chooses to live in the beautiful countryside of Oxford and is unable to get a bus. However, for an agricultural worker, living in the countryside is a necessity and therefore some transport must be provided. Some farmers in Norfolk cope with the mobility of their own people, and their employees are not unduly deprived. It would be interesting to know how this works in Oxfordshire. There are, of course, people who have to work in Oxford and cannot afford to buy a house in the city itself and therefore live in the surrounding villages. Perhaps they are also deprived if the transport services are reduced.

A. WELLS (Berkshire County Council)

Mr. Barrow implies that standards cannot be devised for countywide transport services. Doesn't he think that his council's policy is implicitly basing standards on the demands of pressure groups who can shout the loudest or most effectively to get the services they require? Secondly, could Mr. Barrow possibly explain the composition of parish groups? Are they completely composed of parish councillors?

J.F. BARROW (Oxfordshire County Council)

First, the question of parish councils and pressure groups. The view taken by the county council is that parish councillors are the locally elected representatives at the 'grass roots' of local government. They are most responsive to the needs of local people because they are in closest touch. As elected members they are, and can be, accountable for putting views to the bus companies and to the county council. I do not accept the idea of 'who shouts loudest' succeeding. Indeed I have no evidence that the changes to local bus services which have occurred result from parish councils or groups of parishes acting in an irresponsible way. On the contrary, evidence points to satisfaction with the policy of the council, and the parish council groups have responded constructively and positively to their new role. It is unwise and dangerous to equate parish councils, which are democratically elected bodies, with pressure groups which are not.

As officers, we tried in late 1974 and during 1975 to meet the challenge put to us by county councillors to define social need. Surveys were carried out that are conventionally thought to produce the evidence which leads to definition of social need. It was possible to do so only in very broad terms, and as a static position at the survey date. It was not possible, though, to demonstrate that *precise* social need can be identified at the centre (i.e. at County Hall); nor could a centralized system be produced which would be flexible and responsive enough to deal with the myriad changes which occur weekly or monthly. The council therefore began to form the view that social need is best determined at a more local level through a responsive, accountable organization provided by groups of parishes.

I agree with Dr. Ochojna about defining minimum levels of service. It will be a sad day for local government if minimum levels of service are imposed by central government upon councils. It will further erode the discretion of local government to decide for itself and limit the choice that councils should exercise as elected and accountable authorities.

In Mr. Horam's introduction there was reference to the unreality of central government setting standards, which is heartening. Levels of service should be determined at local level in any way that individual councils feel appropriate for their area, just as councils should be given the opportunity to decide for themselves how they intend to deal with the whole question of rural transport. Councils could and should then be responsible for their individual approaches.

Mr. Lutman may be unhappy with the decision of the Oxfordshire County Council on subsidy, which, as explained before, is based on the view that subsidy will be paid for specific and identifiable socal need. Hopefully there is a positive output from City of Oxford Motor Services of what constitutes their viable network. When the company has completed that study it should be possible for the council to consider, with the bus companies, which are the areas and routes requiring specific support and whether that support should be provided. Subsidy that is paid out to any operator as 'blanket' support is not in accordance with the approach adopted by the Oxfordshire Council and whatever fluctuations might arise in the requests for such general support as a result of different experiences and assumptions about inflation are irrelevant to the issue. The principle that must be emphasized is that a *general* subsidy to any operator is not acceptable to the county council. I have no evidence to share Mr. Lutman's misgivings about what he termed the selfishness of parish groups. If a group should ask for service changes which affect other parishes or groups of parishes there are means whereby groups can consult a liaise before proposals are made. Similarly, discussions can be held on those few occasions where services cross the county boundary. Those occasional events are surely not a major disadvantage to the system which has been devised.

PROFESSOR G.P. WIBBERLEY (University of London)

Mr. Barrow's reply is intriguing. Why is his an optimistic view when all other evidence points to the narrow minded pushing of sectional interests by other countryside pressure groups? Why does he feel that careful and altruistic analysis of the rural transport theme will be given by his parish groups? In my own parish group the introduction of housing associations into the village and new forms of employment cause very prejudiced comments both at parish meetings and at the parish council. Several county planning officers say that their staff should be responsible for interpreting the wishes of the silent people in their counties. Those who are deprived of rural transport are generally people from the lower income group who have usually had to give in to other stronger groups in all other matters.

Mr. Deavin claims that many farmers in Norfolk look after the mobility problems of their workers. Certainly farmers look after their own transport problems and we presume that they look after those of their families and workers; farm workers are generally mobile. However, one of the main reasons why COSIRA (Council for Small Industries in Rural Areas) has put a number of 'advance' factories in to the Lindsey area of Lincolnshire, for example, is to improve at the local level the employment prospects of farm workers' families. This is a good way of approaching the transport problem—trying, as it were, to reduce the problem slightly by producing a choice of a few jobs locally, thus helping to change the situation whereby farmers' children often had to leave their rural community due to lack of employment.

J.F. BARROW

Professor Wibberley has probably fallen into the trap of regarding parish councils as pressure groups. Occasionally one is tempted to ask—to whom are such pressure groups accountable? Who elects them? Who decides on the evidence they will present on a particular issue? Surely there are constitutional differences between such groups and parish councils. The important distinction is that the councils are elected and therefore accountable for their action as part of the democratic system. It would be better to have within that democratic system, decisions taken locally (for example, on standards of service, if elected members want standards); and controversy arising from debate. Is it not a stimulus to the democratic system to have debate about local transport at the parish level? Should not local pressure groups and individuals have the opportunity to pressurize parish councils for local bus services or changes in the services—with the parish council then being accountable for its decision? It is healthy for democracy. To place parish councils in the same category as pressure groups is really denigrating the role of parish councils.

The second theme raised by Professor Wibberley concerns local job opportunity. I agree heartily with what he says. It is appropriate for Structure Plans to have policies which encourage and promote small-scale employment in villages, for the reason he gave. But in the context of Rural Transport and Country Planning small-scale industry located, say, in 'key' villages, will hardly actively help to produce more passengers on public transport. Admittedly the evidence is empirical, but more local industry probably produces greater travel by car between towns and villages and hardly a significant change in the numbers using rural bus services. Small industries in rural areas are favourable but we should not delude ourselves into believing that this will necessarily help rural public transport.

PROFESSOR G.P. WIBBERLEY

I am not concerned with public transport—I am concerned with mobility for rural people, and if they can do it more happily through the private motor car because of a better local employment situation that's fine.

T.S. JAMIESON (Sir Frank Mears & Partners)

With reference to remarks made by Professor Wibberley, the questions of public transport and mobility seems to have become concerned with the need to increase the number of trips by public transport vehicles. In some way it is assumed that this will create more opportunities, greater mobility and better conditions for people in rural areas. In Scotland, this kind of greater mobility invariably results in deterioration of other small-scale services in rural communities. It has resulted in a deterioration in the ability of shops to provide a service, of small industries to provide employment and even of schools to remain open. We have to be aware that in achieving greater mobility there is a danger of reducing the standard of other services which are required in rural communities.

R.A. BROWN (Department of Transport)

Professor Wibberley mentioned the improvements that have occurred in rural communities; perhaps those improvements are partly the result of deliberate subsidy policy, the results of subsidy by nationalized industries, which if they were operating strictly commercially, would not have connected the isolated country cottage with gas, water, electricity, etc. Is there something different about public transport in rural areas? Is public transport itself or the facilities which transport enables rural dwellers to enjoy less basic? If they are not less basic, is subsidy warranted? In education or the health service there are certain minimum standards and yet in the UK we doubt whether a minimum level for public transport is a reasonable criterion. Dr. de Kogel seemed to suggest that in the Netherlands there were basic levels of service necessary for broad social welfare purposes. The contrast is rather distinct. Is it possible to relate the difference in attitude to how rural society is viewed and what kind of rural society is being aimed at? If central direction of transport or land use planning is subordinated to development by pressure of market forces, there is a phasing problem, as people adjust to declining local services or as they shift their employment or house location. Is subsidy warranted to cushion the effects of change?

R.C. WINFIELD (Dyfed County Council)

There is an ongoing household interview survey in the rural areas of Dyfed. In the first pilot study, where there was apparently a good public transport service through the area, the comment received was that people did not want the buses that they had because, although they were frequent, they were not convenient for what people wanted to do. Subsequently, in the area of this study, a once-a-week service has been started specifically tailored for market day and the doctor's surgery and this is both successful and, on a marginal basis, profitable. In further studies in areas where there is no bus service, there has been the same response that people want a specific service, either weekly or even fortnightly, and where these have been laid on they have again been profitable. They have also become an important social event and the county council are generating traffic, not so much for people to get to places but to join social and community events. There is no great merit in travelling for the sake of it, but if people are travelling to enrich their lives, perhaps something is being achieved. By providing an apparently low level of service existing resources can be spread over many more places. Possibly the normally accepted dictum of requiring more frequent buses to provide a better service is incorrect in a rural area. It is a matter of quality rather than quantity.

E.J. CRAWFORD (Kent County Council)

Over three million pounds a year is spent in Kent getting children to school and I would like to ask Dr. de Kogel whether the financial support from the Dutch

36

Government to the bus companies in Holland includes an element that covers this or is there a separate subsidy for school journeys? The educational aspect of the rural bus problem is very much in our minds in Kent.

DR. C.G. DE KOGEL (Joint Management Organization of Regional Bus Operators in the Netherlands)

The public transport subsidy to regional bus companies in the Netherlands is a general subsidy. It is not a summation of different subsidies, for example for educational services, for transport of disabled people, etc.

J.F. BARROW

Mr. Crawford enquired about school transport because it might be an area where there could be greater success than experiments such as car sharing schemes. The Oxfordshire County Council have adopted a system of extended school contracts which aim to provide local bus services associated with the provision of school buses for pupils. Briefly, the council invite tenders for the provision of transport for specified school journeys for pupils, and associate this with the provision of unspecified journeys for a particular locality for which the council will pay a prescribed hourly rate up to a maximum number of hours per week. The parish groups and the bus operators then decide what service will be provided, within the prescribed finances. This system has now been the subject of four tenders from operators which have been accepted by the council. Certainly the greater integration of all forms of transport in rural areas is worth exploration. For instance the provision of transport by area health authorities, social services, education and so on. The expenditure by such bodies must run into several millions of pounds each year in a county such as Oxford. Are the greatest benefits gained from it?

PROFESSOR G.P. WIBBERLEY

Mr. Brown was right to pose the question 'What do we want out of rules for society?' In the past, the nature of rules for society, dominated by certain privileged groups, was wrong. We do not want to return to that situation. Villages are small scale in terms of population and events. Also they contain a mixture of social and economic groups which should ideally encourage both cooperation and tension, which according to sociologists creates a healthy environment. A choice of employment is also important so that there is a local as well as a commuting population. A greater degree of choice should be brought back into rural communities.

Mr. Jamieson is correct in his view that too much opportunity given to rural people, especially in relation to mobility, can tend to disintegrate rural communities. However, the history of rural depopulation shows that though

37

people can be dammed up superficially in rural areas, some will finally get out and go to cities, even if they find no employment, in order to escape from rural segregation. I agree with Mr. Barrow in that the only way forward is for local groups and communities to decide what they want, as long as they do not act in an exclusive way. To return to Mr. Brown's point of view, it is questionable whether it is wise to equalize opportunities in the field of mobility because of the difficulties of judging between desire and need. It is almost impossible to decide.

When in the Ministry of Agriculture, I was asked to make a study of the minor rural road pattern in relation to very isolated farms. I made the suggestion of subsidizing Land Rovers and Jeeps for the farmers who were situated at the end of these unimproved and unclassified roads. This recommendation was turned down and the government proceeded to upgrade these rural roads at great expense. We have an inability to look upon some of these problems as being social welfare ones where perhaps the cheapest and most successful way is the direct way of helping individuals. We tend to opt for the more indirect and expensive solution.

DR. C.G. DE KOGEL

I was impressed by Mr. Winfield's comment about specific services in rural areas. Perhaps I gave the impression that by standardizing the service level we have no specific services in the Netherlands. This is not so. For example, there are services in rural areas to specifically coincide with a market in a nearby town.

Regarding Professor Wibberley's comments on social aspects of transport in rural areas, a study around Emmen in the north emphasized the correlation between the service level of public transport and the level of education in the neighbourhood. Villages with good public transport service connections to the city, where the schools are, had a higher level of education than those without public transport. In another survey, people in rural areas were asked to list, in priority, 20 items, each of which would normally be considered necessary. Very high on that list was a bus service to the nearest town or city.

P. WARMAN (Martin and Voorhees Associates)

Is the drift of this discussion questioning the role of county planning in rural areas? Professor Wibberley suggested that the planner had a role in looking after the interests of the silent majority. Surely this was directed at the lifestyles of people living today. However, just as important is the attempt to plan for future generations who are equally silent.

Planning for the present and future of rural areas should recognize that some diversity and variety in lifestyles is necessary. But the point is what effective influence does the county planner have to enhance this diversity? What

38

instruments of planning are available to him? Apart from transport, he has very few. The control on housing development and shopping is generally responsive, and where local shops are in decline the local authority seldom sees its role as supporting these. Similarly with local employment, its influence for creating rural employment is limited, although the work of COSIRA in this respect may be an example to follow. Provision of health care facilities is not primarily the responsibility of the local authority. If, as in Oxfordshire, planning public transport is left to the wishes only of local parish councils and market forces, the question of whether the county can protect and plan for future generations must be asked.

With regard to the issue of minimum standards of bus service, this is particularly relevant to maintaining the diversity of lifestyles in rural areas. For those without private transport available to them, once the level of service available is described, it is usually very apparent what activities can be engaged in outside the community.

My experience in the context of the study of rural communities in West Yorkshire is that once a service is reduced to less than hourly, the perception of choice of activities involving public transport travel is particularly limited. There is the difficulty of remembering services that are irregular and the outward and return journeys become impossible, say, between breakfast and lunch for a shopping trip, etc. The lack of choice, waiting time and the implications of missing a bus are also a deterrant to relying on less than hourly services. It was noticeable in the Dutch context that the standards being considered for scheduled bus services were a minimum frequency of hourly. Where such a service cannot be provided, the need to consider alternatives to scheduled buses in rural areas is important.

This point is made simply to show that public transport can be considered an instrument of planning policy. Therefore, what is the role of the local government planner in the rural areas and what instruments does he have to implement planning policies other than transport?

G.P. LAWSON (W.S. Atkins Group Ltd.)

What efforts has Mr. Barrow made and what degree of success has he achieved on staggering school and work hours, coordinating the related transport services and generally trying to create other planning instruments to influence the future, given the situation where he is just starting to use transport as a planning instrument.

DR. M. HARRISON (West Yorkshire Passenger Transport Executive)

Mr. Barrow suggests that there should be an initial exploration into the possibility of staggering school and work hours. This is something that has been much talked about and many people say it cannot be done. About 12 months ago, the three secondary schools in Chichester changed their working hours. They had previously all commenced at about 9.00 a.m. and required the operation of some 14 double-deck buses by Southdown Motor Services in addition to the contract services paid for by the county council and the 50 small school buses which the council operates itself. One of the schools now starts at 8.00 a.m. while the other two schools commence at 9.15 a.m. The effect was to reduce the number of buses and the deficit by £70 000 per annum; a significant saving, bearing in mind that the county council subsidy for stage carriage services was of the order of a quarter of a million pounds. Just over half of the school children travelled by stage carriage and contract buses, a third of them travelled by bicycle or walked, 10% by car and 4% by train. The range of their travel times was typically between 15 and 50 minutes, Chichester being set in a rural area.

Mr. Barrow implied that the operators should all do survey work and that if they do not then there is something wrong with them. There is a need for surveys and there are several ways of carrying them out. One is to use ticket machines which have magnetic tape data recorders and this is what a number of operators and county councils are beginning to think of in practical terms. On the other hand, West Yorkshire PTE operates a small survey team costing about £80 000 per annum which is kept running non-stop to review our services, the effect of fare increases and other special studies.

J.F. BARROW

The comments on school hours are interesting. The Oxfordshire education authority tried to introduce the idea of staggering school hours in part of west Oxfordshire with no great success. The reaction from teachers and parents was unfavourable. The failure did not result from want of trying, and efforts will probably be resumed later this year to turn to the staggering of work hours. The initiative in the county council of staggering their own working hours, through 'flexitime', has been taken, partially in the interests of the problems of peak-hour travelling. The efforts with other major employers, mostly in the service sector in the city, have not been wholly successful. Again Oxford will learn from others and make further attempts.

To return to the points raised by Mr. Warman. Planners are not the only people who affect rural areas. Contacts over the years with the Ministry of Agriculture, COSIRA, the public transport operators, the nationalized industries and the private sector show that the influences on rural areas are as manifold and as complex as they are in urban areas. Better means of discussion at local level between all these interests must be found.

40

PROFESSOR G.P. WIBBERLEY

There is so much in the countryside dynamic that is not affected by the statutory planning system. The comment that if planning authorities lose control of rural transport they will, as it were, have a countryside that is on the loose in relation to a planning authority, is just. The planning system handles most of the problems that arise in urban areas but it is singularly unadapted to dynamic rural problems. There are, in fact, in rural areas, a number of different planning systems in competition. The agricultural planning system is one which is based on price signals, with grants or subsidies also being used. The work being done with the development of small industries in rural areas is another type of planning—A man is picked who has already shown that he is capable of starting a small industry and that he is capable of developing it, and then he will be helped. Advance factories are put up, management accounts are brought in and technical advice is given.

Countryside planning is essentially a development problem. The trouble is that planning of the countryside is looked at as if it were a holding job, a restricting operation. The result is that those people who benefit from the *status quo* will benefit from the operation of the existing statutory planning systems whereas those who have got problems, lack jobs and services, gain nothing from it. There is much thought at the moment as to how to create a planning system that is more in line with development possibilities rather than one that is a series of preservation measures.

PART TWO
Rural Transport Policy and Finance

CHAPTER FOUR

Future Rural Transport and Development Policy

Andrew Blowers

Rural transport facilities and resources are inequitably distributed and poorly
coordinated. Consequently certain social groups lack mobility and deeply rural
areas are inaccessible. The immediate goal of rural transport should be to
provide minimum standards of mobility and concessions for the deprived
groups in the population. This can be achieved by better use of existing
resources especially of conventional bus services. The contribution of unconventional services can be useful but is liable to be exaggerated. The reorganization of the bus industry and greater county council control within generally
agreed standards will help to achieve the social welfare goal. Rural development policy should accelerate the trend towards concentration of activities and
opportunities in key centres and positively discriminate in improving the
accessibility of the least mobile groups. In the longer term a reassessment of
policy may be necessary to minimize mobility for all groups in order to conserve
resources.

The Problem

Rural transport is commonly presented as a 'problem'. Explicitly or by
implication it is regarded as a problem for which appropriate 'solutions' should
be sought by the planning authorities. This presupposes that the problem can
be diagnosed, that cures can be found, and, more important, that they should
be applied. There is a tendency to focus on short term incremental changes to
the transport system to improve mobility, rather than to pursue longer term
strategies which relate transport planning to rural development policy to
improve accessibility. It is worthwhile to start from first principles by asking,
what is the problem?

45

The rural transport problem is not, as is often supposed, essentially one of capacity or of finance. Rural areas have a higher car ownership rate than is common in urban areas (70% according to the Green Paper on Transport Policy (4.1)) and in some areas car ownership must be approaching the notional 'saturation' level. The bus mileage operated in rural areas by public transport has only begun to fall significantly during the 1970s (7% reduction 1970-4 (4.2)), whereas the number of passengers has been falling at about 4% per year over a much longer period. In consequence there is considerable spare capacity both in cars and on buses. The problem is the inflexibility of supply to meet the great variation in potential demand for various types of journey from a scattered population of individuals with differing transport needs.

The Transport Policy White Paper, 1977 (4.3) defines the problem thus:

'People living in the country face greater problems than many others in getting about, for the population is sparser and distances they may need to travel are longer and have grown more so as public and other services have become more centralised.'

Financially, rural bus services are to receive continuing support from public funds. This represents a reversal of government policy which would have halved revenue support for buses (urban and rural) by the end of the decade. The White Paper (4.4) on transport commits the government to maintain the overall level of support and within this level to increase the provision for rural services by £15 million by the end of the decade. This confirms the redistribution of subsidy in favour of rural areas already begun, to achieve a substantial shift away from holding down fares in the major conurbations towards the maintenance of levels of service in less populated areas.

Revenue support is, of course, but a fraction of the public sector investment in rural public transport which includes capital grants for infrastructure, bus grant, and fuel subsidy for stage carriage services. In addition local authorities provide school contract services and social service vehicles for the elderly and handicapped. Local authorities subsidize mobility of people through concessionary fares schemes, the provision of transport through revenue support, and try to reduce the need for certain kinds of travel by bringing activities within easier reach of people (e.g. mobile libraries, meals on wheels). Such activities are complemented by provision of works buses and mobile shops and delivery services. Any global calculation of investment in transport in rural areas would also have to take into account road improvements and maintenance, and expenditure on private cars and public transport fares. A calculation undertaken for Norfolk in 1974/5 suggested that direct spending by the public authorities alone on transportation was at least £20 million. Thus the decline in subsidies and the threatened loss of services should be viewed in the context of the resources currently absorbed in rural transport. Indeed, White argues that, 'Even a marginal diversion of resources from highway expenditure in "shire" counties would permit existing service levels to be maintained, and perhaps improved' (4.5). The issue is whether resources are being allocated in the best way to meet the needs of the rural community.

In essence contemporary rural transport is a distributional problem. It is specific rather than general, revealing considerable spatial and social inequalities in mobility and accessibility. Spatially it is a problem of the deeply rural areas without access to conventional inter urban bus services. Socially it is a problem affecting those who are unable through age, disability or income to possess and drive a car. These social and spatial aspects of the problem were well summed up in a report on rural transport in West Suffolk, 'But the main problem in many areas is ceasing to be one of public transport. Rather it is one of catering for a residuum consisting of the needs of a small minority of the population, too dispersed any longer to justify conventional bus services but very real needs none the less' (4.6).

There are also quite arbitrary inequalities arising through historical and political circumstances. Fare levels and concessions and the density of rural services differ markedly between and within counties as a result of the financial circumstances of the operators or the policies pursued by operators or local authorities. Given the discretion now exercised towards public transport by county councils under their Section 203 powers and their relative freedom to use Transport Supplementary Grant (TSG) within well defined PESC limits, different political philosophies are being expounded in their Transport Policies and Programmes (TPPs). Indeed, the unwillingness of some non-metropolitan county councils to support unremunerative bus services resulted in only £34 million of the £41 million allocated in the TSG for revenue support being used for that purpose in 1976-77. To take two extreme cases: Bedfordshire aim to introduce 'measures to improve public transport to provide safe, convenient, reliable and regular services' (4.7) and to provide the necessary financial support for this purpose, whereas Oxfordshire have adopted the principle that, 'It is for all public transport companies in the County so to organize and operate their bus services so that the best practicable service is provided for the public without subsidy by the County Council' (4.8).

A major obstacle to the achievement of generally acceptable and applicable solutions to rural transport· and development problems is the plethora of agencies involved. There has been a tendency to 'market segmentation' (4.9) which has resulted in lack of coordination and underuse of resources. This can partly be solved by better management within county councils, but part of the problem is outside their control. The overall responsibility of the county councils for transportation and strategic planning through their TPPs and Structure Plans, gave birth to hopes for better coordination which quickly

E   47 became stillborn when the realities of continuing conflict over planning with the district councils and the lack of effective powers in the area of public transport became apparent. The ultimate weakness of planning in a mixed economy is its lack of powers of implementation. Behind it all is the prevailing social structure with its inequalities of class and power which no amount of coordination by agencies established as part of that structure can do much to alter.

The problem we face, then, is of inequalities in mobility and accessibility experienced by particular groups in specific locations. It is compounded by inequalities relating to political differences and historical circumstances and by the lack of coordination between agencies at the local level. It is a problem that requires redistribution of finance and transport resources. There is no lack of research, experiment or policies for rural transport. What is lacking is an overall perspective which places the rural transport problem in its social and spatial context. Such a perspective requires the logical connection to be made between those objectives which are directed towards rural transport and those which relate to rural development. The achievement of a coherent and consistent strategy varied in detail to accord with local circumstances must begin from an understanding of the processes at work in the rural area which are shaping its future.

Trends of Rural Development

Two related trends have been at work in rural areas over a long period. These are the growth in car ownership and the tendency towards concentration of activities and opportunities in the larger or more accessible settlements. These trends have encouraged the withdrawal of rural bus services. The National Travel Survey revealed that 'each additional car had caused the number of bus trips per annum to fall by 450 in 1964 and by only 300 in 1972, reflecting the lower level of public transport usage and the fact that a greater proportion of the additional cars were going to households already owning at least one car' (4.10). As rationalization of bus services proceeds so the public transport network becomes increasingly confined to inter urban services serving larger villages *en route*. Although rural activities and opportunities have become more concentrated rural populations have remained dispersed partly because of the higher mobility enjoyed by some groups, and partly through inertia. Some adjustment is now taking place as planning policies aimed at greater concentration of population in rural areas begin to take effect. The overall effects of these trends are described in the Green Paper,

'In some areas, particularly in country areas where public transport has been most extensively reduced, the opportunities for mobility of people without access to a car are lower now than they have been for a generation or more. Yet at the same time as mobility has been reduced for those without a car, its advantages have increased. For as car ownership spreads, schools become larger, hospitals are regionalised, out-of-town shopping centres multiply and the council offices are situated further away; meanwhile the local shop and post office have disappeared. Mobility becomes ever more necessary; but command over it for the minority becomes less' (4.11).

The size of the minority varies and may be disputed. The West Suffolk and Devon surveys (4.12) found only 6% using public transport frequently and half rarely or never using it. Viewed another way, that those families without cars are entirely dependent on public transport and that one car families are partially dependent, the level of potential deprivation seems quite high. Many parishes in Bedfordshire had over 70% partially dependent on this basis (4.13). Clearly it is possible to underestimate or to exaggerate the problem depending on the method of calculation. It appears that in many rural areas car ownership rates are now so high that any further satisfaction of mobility needs in rural areas must come from public transport. A second car may be regarded as an essential burden and inadequacy of rural public transport could not only maintain this burden but also continue to draw heavily on national oil reserves. In certain circumstances a poorly used public transport network in rural areas is likely to prove less economic in the use of fuel than alternatives such as the use of shared cars. In the rural areas there is a clear divide between those who have personal mobility which gives them access to a range of opportunities and those who must face either longer, more expensive and inconvenient journeys, even for basic necessities, or become increasingly dependent on social services, or on voluntary and self help transport schemes.

In the longer term, forms of cooperation already present in rural society may evolve further to ameliorate the problems of those deprived of private transport. Greater sharing of private cars might develop and the White Paper proposes relaxing present controls. Systems of communal production or purchase of essential commodities might proliferate. But, such trends are, by their nature, likely to be too sporadic or inadequate to offer hope of any general solution to rural transport problems.

Changes in leisure habits and in working hours may increase the opportunities for the more mobile groups but are unlikely to permeate the whole population for some time. The development of telecommunications may increasingly free certain groups of workers from the rigidity of office hours but is likely to be a complement to personal travel not a substitute for it. The one countervailing tendency to increasing disparities between the mobile and those deprived of personal transport could be the need for energy conservation and the rapidly increasing costs of motoring. This could depress the amount of travel by private transport and increase the demand for alternatives less wasteful of scarce resources. A shift in public opinion against high expenditure on roads and the vehicle industry and in favour of policies to reduce mobility and preserve environment would also contribute to any reversal of present trends. But the perceived costs in terms of time, convenience and price of motoring as against any alternatives will have to be very high before a transfer from one mode to another on a substantial scale is likely to occur. Finally, as the tendency for facilities and people to become concentrated in those areas with greatest accessibility continues, the isolation of those without personal transport who remain in the deeply rural areas will increase. It will become difficult to distinguish between those who choose to live there and those who have little choice.

The Goals of Rural Policy

Two concepts are significant when elaborating the goals of rural transport and development policy. These are *mobility* and *accessibility*. Mobility is a function of transport and describes an individual's propensity or ability to travel whereas accessibility depends on location relative to a defined range of activities and opportunities. Accessibility can be altered by changes in location of activities and in the transport system.

Mobility

In the broadest terms the goal of rural transport policy should focus on meeting the needs and demands for mobility of the rural population. This would embrace all groups in the population and clearly the cost of provision requires priorities to be set. The Green Paper suggests the goal should be to give higher priority to the social welfare aspects of transport, and in particular to the public transport needs of those without access to a car. The emphasis should be on need rather than demand, and the priority groups would seem to be the elderly, the young, the disabled, and those who cannot afford or cannot drive a car. The White Paper reaffirms this approach emphasizing a selective approach to subsidies in order to secure a fairer distribution of income as well as value for money. It warns:

'To use subsidies to disguise from people the cost of the services they are paying for is pointless, and to subsidise richer people at the expense of poorer is perverse.'

Of less concern will be those groups who might use public transport as a stand-by or as an alternative to their own transport. Each group has specific travel needs (shopping, work, entertainment, medical) although some could be accommodated by a transport service designed for multiple purpose journeys.

50

Accessibility

A second broad goal would be to achieve a minimum level of accessibility for each settlement. Such a goal would seek to shape the pattern of distribution of activities and services to provide opportunities in housing, employment, shopping, medical services and leisure so as to meet the needs of the less mobile groups in the population. Obviously these goals are interrelated and include short term adaptations of transport services and longer term changes in the location of activities and population.

Societal goals

There are other goals, too, affecting society as a whole which might be applied to rural areas. Goals of environmental and resource conservation may be complementary to social welfare policies directed towards specific groups. For instance, a policy of concentrating population could reduce travel needs, improve accessibility, save energy, and protect the countryside. On a broader front still the level of deprivation might be reduced by adopting social goals relating to income distribution, housing, minimum standards of welfare etc. which are beyond the range of this chapter. Here two areas of policy applicable to rural areas will be concentrated on—transport policies to improve mobility for deprived groups, and location policies designed to improve accessibility in rural areas.

Improving Mobility

Concessionary fares

The social welfare goal of greater mobility may be achieved either by policies directed towards specific social groups or by policies to provide specific types of transport service. Policies for groups include subsidies for individuals, the most common of which are concessionary fare schemes for the elderly and disabled and bus passes or contract vehicles for school children. The latter are mandatory for children living more than three miles (4.8 km) from the nearest appropriate school (two miles (3.2 km) for children under eight). Concessionary fare schemes are discretionary and vary according to the area and distance covered, the amount of concession granted, and the period for which it is available. The Green Paper discovered that 60 out of 333 district councils had no scheme at all operating.

The wide disparities in the provision of fares concessions between one local authority and another seem unfair to many of those who are statutorily eligible for concessions.' (4.14)

Only Bedfordshire, of the non-metropolitan counties, has a county wide free fare

51

system (up to 14 miles (22.5 km)) for the elderly and disabled (4.15). There is a strong case for applying a minimum national standard to concessionary fares to help overcome the arbitrary inequalities that currently exist.

Conventional bus services

Subsidies to individuals are of little use if there is no service on which to use them. More use could probably be made of school contract vehicles for fare paying passengers using Section 30 (1968 Transport Act) permits and some staggering of school hours would provide better use of the fleet. But the best immediate hope lies in the maintenance and improvement of the conventional bus system which, despite cuts, remains extensive (Fig. 4.1). This will require the removal of uncertainty by a commitment at central and local government level to provide the necessary support.

Bedfordshire decided to underwrite its level of services, at first without support from central government through the Transport Supplementary Grant (TSG). In the first years after reorganization economies and service changes consistent with this policy were made in cooperation with the bus company. A much stronger base was created from which improvements and innovations could take effect. In the rural areas a detailed study of rural transport needs and resources using local volunteers is being undertaken for

Figure 4.1   Typical rural conventional bus service (Bedfordshire County Council)

each of nine sectors into which the county is divided. The surveys have two objectives, (i) 'The identification of areas where a minimum level of provision is lacking' and (ii) 'The identification of improvements to better match existing resources to changing patterns of demand' (4.16). Among the alterations and improvements which have been introduced are the retiming and diversions of existing services and additional morning, evening and Sunday services. The use of school contract vehicles under Section 30 permits or 'dead runs' have provided services to villages off the main routes and a free service to a doctor's surgery (since withdrawn). Among the innovations have been a commuter bus and a 'drop-me-off' service (the 'Nightrider') leaving Bedford at 22.45 hours every Friday on a route determined by the destination of its passengers (Fig. 4.2). Other flexible services on the lines of the highly successful Leighton-Linslade Midibus principle (flat fare, stop anywhere (4.17) or the Eastern Counties Omnibus Company's Huntingdon scheme could be introduced in more densely populated areas (Fig. 4.3). Such innovations and adaptations to existing services meet a variety of needs—the journey to work, shopping, medical, and leisure—for various groups—the elderly, the young, housewives and commuters. Concentration on better use of existing resources can bring considerable social benefits.

Unconventional services

It seems prudent to concentrate on improving the existing network before embarking on unconventional and voluntary schemes. Many authorities seem to have embraced the concepts of post bus, community bus, dial-a-ride, car sharing, taxi and car hire schemes. A variety of projects are in existence (4.18). Some, like the Huntingdon Midibus scheme have been developed by the operator, some are the fruits of partnerships involving operator, county council and local community (the Norfolk Village Bus being the most well known example), and others are entirely local initiatives like the Horncastle Bus Club. The Department of Transport have established a series of experiments in Devon, North Yorkshire, South Ayreshire and Dyfed (4.19) to investigate use of existing services and the potential of unconventional services. Considering the significance of conventional rural services and the number of existing unconventional schemes already in operation the Department's efforts might be better employed in monitoring existing service levels and experiments. It has to be recognized that unconventional services are not of themselves answers to the rural transport problem although the naive optimism placed in them in some quarters may suggest otherwise. They may help to fill gaps in the conventional network but maintaining them once the initial enthusiasm has subsided may be difficult. Very often the local leadership and voluntary effort on which some of these services depend is lacking in those areas most in need. Dependence on voluntary services introduces issues of dependence on others and incongruence

Figure 4.2   The 'Nightrider' drop-me-off service preparing to leave Bedford bus station (Bedfordshire County Council)

Figure 4.3   The Leighton-Linslade 'Midibus'   (Bedfordshire County Council)

of life styles that may leave a minority still deprived. At worst voluntary schemes may become 'amateurish lift-giving schemes which carry echoes of paternalism and charity long since rejected in urban areas' (4.20). The establishment of parish groups as suggested by Oxfordshire, the appointment of officers to coordinate and initiate local transport schemes, and the payment of car drivers or even a subsidy for the purchase of a car to isolated households may each contribute to ensuring social needs are met.

Minimum standards

The notion of establishing minimum standards of mobility has been criticized on the grounds that they would be too crude and insensitive to the variety of local conditions. They would be difficult to apply unless set at a very general and low level. Conversely, if high standards were established resources might have to be diverted from other desirable social policies in order to meet them. Unless standards of some kind are established inconsistency and inequality in rural transport will persist. Standards have been established for a whole range of services provided at local level, whether mandatory in the case of education, or discretionary as with certain social services, and there is nothing intrinsically different about rural transport when viewed as a part of social welfare policy. If common national criteria for judging the socially acceptable minimum levels of service can be formulated and adopted this will still leave a great deal of discretion to the local community in applying them.

The White Paper expresses concern about the differences in concessionary fares schemes and the government intends to explore ways of eliminating differential fares within the same area which result from operators conforming to different financial disciplines. But its concern does not extend to the view that national standards or guidelines on concessionary fares, fare levels and bus services are feasible or desirable. Minimum standards of service levels are the most difficult to judge and it has to be admitted that the variation of geographical and social circumstances makes it highly unlikely that a simple formula will be found. The government has, however, indicated in its TSG allocations that it will give special weight to proposals aimed at maintaining minimum levels of public transport service particularly in less densely populated areas. Some areas have already suggested certain minimum levels of public transport provision. Guidelines proposed or adopted show considerable variation and in view of this the National Bus Company have commissioned a study to assess whether certain specific 'levels' (or standards) of service can be established as a minimum requirement in areas having particular spatial, population and other characteristics.

Examples of guidelines for rural transport services demonstrate a variety in approach. Kent County Council propose a 'minimum standard of mobility' in rural areas of 'at least one or two off-peak services per week to the nearest urban centre' (4.21). East Sussex, in their Structure Plan, suggested that within 0.9 miles (1.5 km) of every settlement of 100 or more people there should be a daily service for schools and at least a weekly service connecting to other centres. Bedfordshire has adopted a set of population thresholds for six types of journey. A settlement of 50 or more population would have a weekly shopping service; at a population of a 100, work journeys should be provided; at 200 a service to a doctor's surgery is considered justifiable; and at 500 daily shopping services, and late evening and Sunday services should be introduced where they do not exist at present. It needs to be stressed that these are guidelines and that factors such as levels of car ownership, the mobile and fixed provision of services within villages, the geographical and demographic structure of the settlement and the cost of provision (it is suggested that any service should normally cover at least 25% of its cost) would have to be incorporated in a more sophisticated index when applied locally. Nonetheless, these guidelines correspond fairly well to the needs of settlements as revealed by survey and they can be met, at least in Bedfordshire, substantially through adjustments to the conventional bus network. Standards applied nationally would need to define the frequency and type of service, perhaps with a minimum level of cost to be met from fares. They should be sufficiently flexible to take account of local geography, demographic structure, car ownership levels and the availability of local shops and other facilities.

Improving Accessibility

Accessibility within the rural area can be achieved through development policies. Policies aimed to concentrate rural activities at key centres are now well established, whether as a measure to restrain dispersal and thus conserve resources and preserve village character in areas of population growth or to anticipate decline and regroup activities for economic reasons as in, for example, County Durham. The implementation of such policies has been criticized for failing to appreciate their impact on the social structure, and community feeling in rural areas (4.22). However, they have been established long enough to become in many instances, self fulfilling prophecies. The costs to the public sector of providing services on a dispersed basis are likely to prove prohibitive and in the private sector small units (shops, pubs) are being closed as they fail to compete with the services provided in larger settlements. Planning policies are tending to reinforce these trends.

Although a basic transport service for remote areas may be maintained it cannot provide the less mobile with the opportunities enjoyed in larger settlements. Changes in opening hours and the introduction of peripatetic multipurpose service centres (including library, shops and medical facilities) may reduce the inconvenience and isolation felt in such areas. In the long run the disparities in service and transport provision may have to be explicitly recognized and built in to welfare policies. Local authorities through their Structure Plans and using the Community Land Act may try to restrict still further the development of less accessible areas and concentrate resources, including council housing, especially for the elderly, in those villages supplied with services and accessible from the surrounding area and connected to larger settlements by public transport.

Such policies will encourage the tendency for more remote villages to be occupied by those with private transport. Increasing social segregation will occur within rural areas. Given the long standing decline of rural employment opportunities and services, a deliberate policy of moving the less mobile to the most accessible villages may prove the most acceptable development policy. If social welfare goals are to be achieved in the long run it seems most practicable to discriminate in favour of those groups which are most deprived in terms of mobility and accessibility. The goal of accessibility is thus best achieved by maintaining the trend of concentration while the goal of mobility can be secured by a range of transport policies designed to bring services to the people or to move people to the services. The goals and standards of rural transport and development policy can provide the framework within which policies designed to meet them making better use of existing resources can be established. The scope of such policies has been outlined in this paper.

Current Problems

It is easy to ignore current difficulties when considering the possibilities of future development. The public transport industry is passing through a financial crisis. This crisis has been met by a combination of fare increases, service rationalizations and cuts, and increased demands for subsidy, all of which have worsened the position of the passengers. The differing financial position of the operators produces variations in the incidence of subsidy demands between and within counties. Indiscriminate subsidies can obscure the true economic costs and social benefits of alternative services. What needs to be questioned is not the principle of subsidy but its application.

On the question of fares there is increasing evidence that the conventional wisdom that price is a relatively insignificant factor in attracting or maintaining ridership is open to challenge. White reports cases where a rise in fares of 15% in real terms resulted in a fall in passengers of 10% in 1975 and one where a rise was self-defeating in that no extra revenue resulted (1976) (4.23). He argues that for certain groups (e.g. families) and in rural areas fares elasticities may be higher since the proportion of non work journeys undertaken

57

can be reduced in response to higher fares. In any event a loss of passengers, however small, represents a social cost which is borne by those groups with little alternative to travel by bus.

If county councils are to have the ability and the will to implement rural transport policies they will need to have greater powers than they have at present. In terms of the White Paper greater control over local public transport is to be given to the transportation authorities and with it the freedom to determine their own policies. Each authority will be required to produce a county public transport plan. This will place the onus firmly on the local authorities. Given the considerable variation of attitudes to public transport found among transportation authorities it remains to be seen whether these plans will produce in every case the kind of stability and imaginative development the government is looking for in public transport.

A view seems to be emerging that the counties should take over the licensing from the Traffic Commissioners. This need not mean a free for all which might threaten the stability and variability of conventional services and possibly result in uneconomic competition. Counties should be obliged to pay regard to the provision of the most effective and economic system to meet their transportation objectives. Some freeing of existing regulations for carriage of fare paying passengers in small vehicles may help in specific instances where it does not erode an existing socially beneficial service. Such changes in licensing law are foreshadowed in the White Paper but the government do not intend to transfer licensing functions to the county councils and consider that separate and independent Traffic Commissioners should be retained since they are best suited to deal with traffic crossing county and regional boundaries. However, the Traffic Commissioners will have to have regard in future to transportation authorities' policies and plans for local transport.

Greater county council involvement implies more control over existing operators will be necessary. The government intend local authorities to enter into binding arrangements with operators for those services which require support but do not propose to make any radical changes in the existing structure of public transport operation. There are persuasive arguments against any move to devolve the NBC and to reorganize its boundaries to conform to those of the counties, notably that it will cause disruption, result in the loss of organizational economies and standards, and lead to increasing inequalities as counties pursue different philosophies. Retaining the advantages of a national organization and at the same time increasing the power of representative authorities to implement their policies are not necessarily incompatible. Provided that consistent policies were assured through the adoption of national criteria on concessions, fares and service levels, there is every reason to think that such a move would produce more responsive and equitable policies at the local level.

Conclusions

It has been argued that the rural transport problem relates to mobility and accessibility. It is both a *social* issue in that it affects groups in the population who lack mobility and a *spatial* issue in that certain parts of the rural area are increasingly inaccessible. There is some evidence to suggest that lack of mobility or accessibility is related to a more general social dissatisfaction in rural areas. Hoare, on the basis of a survey of commuter villages in the hinterland of Norwich, reached the conclusion that 'significant improvements in transport services might well reduce at one and the same time the force of criticism over transport provision and over social hardship' (4.24). Yet it would be unwise to overemphasize the problem and to be distracted from more serious social problems that exist among the disadvantaged groups in cities as well as villages.

In the short run rural mobility can be improved by the adaptation and coordination of existing facilities and resources and there is considerable scope for better use of conventional bus services. Providing a minumum agreed level of service for those dependent on public transport would seem an equitable solution. In the longer term as the concentration of activities and opportunities in urban centres and in key villages continues or is accelerated through planning policies, the deliberate encouragement of the least mobile to move out of the deeply rural areas may be necessary. Eventually the majority of those living in remote villages may be there through choice rather than necessity, regarding its compensations as outweighing the benefits of greater accessibility.

The alternative to this scenario suggests a reversal of current trends. The emphasis could shift dramatically towards reducing mobility, conserving energy and resources, creating local self sufficiency and reducing the degree of specialization and concentration in the economy. Such a shift would require a complete reexamination of our rural transport and development policy. This chapter has focused on policies to accommodate a continuation of current trends. Alternative possibilities should not be discounted. 'The trouble with prolongation of a tendency is that the reversal of the tendency is not anticipated' (4.25). The planner's task is to promote and anticipate change, not merely to react to it.

References

4.1   *Transport Policy, A Consultation Document*, **1,** HMSO, 1976
4.2   *Ibid*
4.3   *Transport Policy*, Cmnd 6836, HMSO, June 1977
4.4   *Ibid*
4.5   WHITE, P.R., *Planning for Public Transport*, Hutchinson, 1976
4.6   DEPARTMENT OF THE ENVIRONMENT, *Study of Rural Transport in West*

Suffolk, Report by the Steering Group, HMSO, 1971

4.7 BEDFORDSHIRE COUNTY COUNCIL, *Transport Policies and Programme 1976-77,* 1975

4.8 OXFORDSHIRE COUNTY COUNCIL, *Local Transport in Oxfordshire,* 1976

4.9 PEDERSON, P.O., *Rural Transport Research in Denmark,* Fifth Annual Seminar on Rural Public Transport, Polytechnic of Central London, 1976

4.10 MITCHELL, C.G.B., Some Social Aspects of Public Passenger Transport, Symposium on Unconventional Bus Services, Transport and Road Research Laboratory 1976

4.11 *Transport Policy, op. cit.*

4.12 DEPARTMENT OF THE ENVIRONMENT, *op. cit;* and *Study of Rural Transport in Devon,* Report of the Steering Group, 1971

4.13 VOORHEES, A.M. and ASSOCIATES, 'In calculating the number of people with some dependence on public transport, all the families which own more than one car and the driver in one car owning families are not included', *Public Transport in Bedfordshire,* 1974

4.14 *Transport Policy, op. cit.*

4.15 Since the change in control of the County Council in 1977 a flat charge of £5 per annum has been introduced for concessionary bus passes.

4.16 BEDFORDSHIRE COUNTY COUNCIL, *Bedfordshire Rural Transport Study,* 1976

4.17 'Big Success for Small Town Services', *Motor Transport,* Bus and Coach Supplement, 17 September 1976

4.18 NATIONAL COUNCIL OF SOCIAL SERVICES, *Rural Transport, 1976,* 1976—This gives a survey by county of rural transport schemes in existence

4.19 *Report on Rural Transport Experiments,* TRRL Symposium on Unconventional Bus Services, 1976

4.20 WHITE, P.R., 'A Review of Rural Transport Developments in 1974/5', *Fourth Annual Seminar on Rural Public Transport,* Polytechnic of Central London, 1975

4.21 KENT COUNTY COUNCIL, *County Structure Plan, Written Statement, Consultative Draft,* 1977

4.22 BLOWERS, A.T., 'Social Planning: the declining villages of County Durham', *New Trends in Geography,* The Open University, 1972; and McLOUGHLIN, B.P., 'Rural Settlement Planning: a new approach', *Town and Country Planning,* March 1976

4.23 WHITE, P.R., 'Response to Recent Fare Increases', *op. cit.;* and with HEELS, P. 'Effect of Changes in Bus Fares on Rural Inter Urban and Small Town Services', *Fifth Annual Seminar on Rural Public Transport,* Polytechnic of Central London, 1976

4.24 HOARE, A.G., 'Some Aspects of the Rural Transport Problem', *Journal of Transport Economics and Policy,* May 1975

4.25 JOUVENAL, B., *The Art of Conjecture,* Weidenfeld and Nicholson, 1967

CHAPTER FIVE

Financing the Rural Bus

Guy Neely

Many aspects of transport planning are common to rural and urban situations. Indeed, often transport services serve both rural and urban functions and this is usually the case with the so called rural bus. Therefore, those buses running through rural areas carry passengers to and from towns and between urban areas as well as on wholly rural journeys. There are dangers in viewing public transport services as a series of distinct and simple stereotypes and possibly some of the mistakes and problems of railway reshaping under Beeching (5.1) and local government reorganization (5.2), arise from the administrative mind trying to straight-jacket transport into a Procrustean bed.

Even so, it is accepted that there are different problems both in terms of costs incurred by transport and the revenue which it can earn in less densely populated areas. Costs and revenue of such services and networks can be considered separately while realising that, in practice, they are inter-dependent. Where there is a deficit between the revenue received from the passengers and the costs incurred, it is necessary to consider what justification there is for someone other than the passenger providing the difference and, finally, how the mechanics of providing that difference can be made to work in practice.

The questions arising from this would seem to be:-

(i) how much bus service should be provided in rural areas?
(ii) what does it cost to provide that which ought to be provided?
(iii) how much ought the passenger to pay at the time he boards his bus?
(iv) how much and for what reasons ought others to pay and how are these sums to be collected?

How Much Ought to be Provided?

It is important to recognize that rural styles of life differ from those in towns in several fundamental respects and not to apply thoughtlessly urban criteria to rural circumstances. One of these differences is the level of transport services.

61

This is nothing new, indeed the process of urbanization has gone hand in hand with the main developments in transport technology. On the other hand, in the past, there were countless hamlets that were without any form of public transport. For many years the population of rural areas has been declining and although this trend is reversing in some areas, the combination of low population densities and higher than average car-ownership mean that the demand for bus transport in rural areas is often too sparse to merit a reasonable service.

Many people regard buses as an insurance against their cars breaking down. This may be one of the reasons why so many more people ask for a village bus than actually use that bus when it has been provided. Or again, the non-users may want the bus for a user on whom they may be dependent; which is a point very much to be borne in mind when, later in this chapter, the reasons why non users should pay for buses are discussed. This paradox of the rural dweller wanting a reasonable public transport service to hand yet not using it sufficiently to keep it busy is a basic problem for rural bus planning. Unlike radio or television, public transport cannot be simply turned on instantly to satisfy demand where and when it arises.

Clearly, some public transport must be provided in less densely populated areas for school children and non drivers who would otherwise be restricted to areas which happened to have easy access to public transport. But we have to recognize bluntly that mobility in rural areas is best provided by the pedestrian, by the cyclist and by the motorist. In urban, inter-urban or suburban areas the bus is definitely not simply the vehicle for the poor, the elderly and the disabled. It has a major, not an ancillary role to play. On the other hand, in truly rural areas, the bus must sometimes be seen, as must the railway, as an assistant for specialist provision, not as a general carrier. But if the rural bus were a truly specialist carrier, it would not be public transport. There is a mixture of roles with social, community and commercial components. A specification of these roles, difficult though it may be, is needed to provide a logical basis for financing rural public transport.

At this point, the approach of this chapter has widened to some extent into a discussion, not simply of financing rural buses but of financing rural transport, in which scene rural buses play a minor role. But it is necessary to recognize that, in many depopulated areas, buses play little part in the movement of people, other than of school children, and never have done.

The final decision on how far each rural bus services should be financed, or subsidized, if it is making a loss, rests with the county council concerned through its annual Transport Policy and Programme (TPP), prepared under the requirements of Section 203 of the Local Government Act 1972 (5.3). The 1977 Transport Policy White Paper gives every encouragement that further finance will be made available for rural buses through the TPP system (5.4).

Costing

The major cost of bus services is labour. In 1976 this represented some 72% of the National Bus Company's overall working expenses (Table 5.1). In the case of rural services, this percentage is likely to be even higher with the operation of smaller buses as labour costs remain relatively inflexible.

TABLE 5.1   National Bus Company Working Expenses

Working Expenses	1974 £000	£000	1975 £000	£000	1976 £000	£000
Operating expenses						
Drivers and conductors	107 588		142 758		153 768	
Fuel, tyres and vehicle licence duties	19 917		21 782		25 850	
Other	11 610		15 454		16 534	
		739 115		179 994		196 152
Maintenance of vehicles						
Repairs	34 156		49 552		57 527	
Depreciation—PSV's	8 721		8 612		8 579	
		42 877		58 164		66 106
Other expenses (e.g. traffic staff, repairs to buildings etc)		56 341		75 360		82 855
		838 333		313 518		345 113
Approximate analysis of working expenses	%		%		%	
Salaries, wages, national insurance and pensions	70		72		72	
Fuel, including duty, and vehicle licence duties	7		5		6	
Other expenses	19		19		19	
Depreciation	4		4		3	
	100		100		100	

Source: National Bus Company Annual Reports 1974, 1975 and 1976

Some aspects of labour costs need particular clarification. A man or woman is needed to drive the public service vehicle. If the vehicle is to be regularly used, more than one man or woman must be assigned to the vehicle to cover days-off, holidays, sickness or the many other reasons for which people absent themselves from work. Even the driver who works a good deal of overtime, will frequently not put in an appearance on more than 270 days in any year. Yet bus services are expected to run on almost every day of the year.

So each public service vehicle will require more than one driver. One might ask, why not do as many shops do and employ part time labour? Again, this in theory is highly plausible. Moonlighting is becoming increasingly fashionable. But driving a bus in many differing conditions requires considerable skill and application. Moreover as the safety of the travelling public is continuously and immediately at stake standards must be high. Though extension of part time work is attractive it has its drawbacks as there has to be a hardcore of full-timers on whom part timers can build. This means, in effect that any bus running a normal schedule and covering 20 000 to 30 000 miles (32 000 to 48 000 km) a year may require more than one full-time driver.

A driver is now a costly person, if one adds to the average industrial wage the national insurance contribution, the uniform, and possibly a pension and subsistence allowance, to say nothing of training costs and sick pay.

To return now to the argument of part time labour. It might be possible to argue that one driver should spend only some of his working week on rural routes and the rest on urban routes, thus being only a part time rural driver. This in fact frequently happens. Therefore, on a strict time apportionment, not all of his wage will be attributable to the rural route. Alternatively, it can be argued that the driver can do other things when he is not driving, such as cleaning the bus, maintaining it or writing up the books. The trouble with this latter breed of man is that not too frequently does he yield up 40 years service to driving buses. He tends, if of an independent frame of mind, to discontinue such work and need replacement. The small man clearly has, and always has had, a big part to play in the provision of rural bus services. Equally, the larger unit which can provide Driver B, when Driver A goes to other employment or goes sick, is also necessary.

Yet the costs of the rural bus do not start and end with the driver. The bus must be maintained. It may require any one of 12 000 spare parts to keep it in good running order. It needs to be cleaned and not all of the maintenance functions can be carried out by a small garage lacking sophisticated equipment. It is true, again, that maintenance costs of rural buses, which are less brutally used by passengers, and run in less arduous traffic conditions, are often smaller than those of their urban cousins. All of us know, however, how much a car costs these days to be maintained. It is not possible to escape the minimum maintenance costs of a bus and even the smallest and most economical operator can reckon on requiring £1000 a year for this purpose. In 1976, the 19 541 buses of the NBC cost £57 527 000 to maintain; an average of £2944 for each bus (5.5).

The third area of cost is, of course, administration, using this word in its widest possible sense. Today, few can move without official documents of some sort. In the case of a bus, a licence, a certificate of fitness, an insurance policy, a ticket machine, a time-table, a fare table, to name but a few, cost time and money. The simple act of employing one man is expensive and time-consuming, even to the extent of working out his PAYE liability. Administration is a growth industry and rural buses have not been exempt from it.

Lastly, of course, there is the cost of the bus itself and of its propulsion. Even a minibus can cost well over £4000 to purchase. The cost of fuel, whatever the vehicle, to cover 30 000 miles (48 000 km) a year has to be reckoned with.

Various means can be tried to reduce the cost of running rural buses. Use of part time drivers or of full time drivers only part time on rural routes has been mentioned. Use of part time vehicles is also becoming fashionable and it is perhaps sensible to examine briefly their economics.

Where wheeled vehicles follow a similar route and have a similar type of timing to that which a bus might have, it can make some sense to combine the carriage of passengers with the carriage of goods or mail. This after all, is the logic behind the carriage of parcels on rural buses. In certain areas the reverse can work and post buses, carrying passengers, have a use. Although limited, in the very sparsely populated areas, this can provide a minimal public transport service where otherwise none at all would exist. Where they have little relevance is when the delivery pattern of letters and parcels is totally different from the flow of traffic. In a Swiss valley both are frequently forced to follow the same route so that their combination on occasions makes sense. This is not always the case in rural England, nor can it be made so.

Similarly, the village bus driven by voluntary labour or the use of a community car scheme has again a part to play, but sometimes a limited part. The hidden cost of training the labour, of seeing that volunteers turn up at 10 o'clock on a cold Sunday night, of seeing that their replacements are available when sickness occurs or that standby vehicles are called in when accidents happen, all these incur real costs, but schemes of this sort can persuade the community to contribute collectively in kind where its members may not be prepared to contribute individually in cash.

A further economy often suggested is the use of a minibus. The problem is here that, whereas a double-decker bus has often the ability—albeit clumsily— to perform the functions of a minibus, the reverse is not true. A double-decker can operate as a mass carrier at peak times on busy routes and also on lightly used off-peak services, whereas the minibus can discharge this latter function satisfactorily; but to attempt the first would mean too many disappointed customers late for work.

Oddly enough, a 70 seat double-decker is therefore more flexible than a 16 seat minibus or its costs are lower than the cost of 4 or 5 minis would be if they had at peak hours to do the work of the double-decker. Further, once the double-decker has been bought, it is sensible to run it for a 12-year period even if by, say, year six the need for its 70 seats has disappeared.

However where there are no large loads, as is often the case in the most rural areas, the minibus has advantages. Its slightly lower costs, compatibility with narrow country roads and low bridges and more intimate character can offer significant advantages in some situations.

In short, several economy measures to the basic cost of running rural buses, which are labour, maintenance, fuel, administration and the cost of the bus itself, can and have been tried. But many of them are palliatives which are either of a specialized or a short lived nature. There is no universal solution to the problem of providing seats at all times for too few bottoms.

Revenue

Where is the money to come from? The most obvious source is the passenger and for many years the passenger has provided the finance for bus services through the 'fare box'. Possibly there have always been voices crying in the wilderness for free fares. The point is that they have usually been crying in the wilderness. Even Herbert Morrison recognized the need for the fare paying passenger to cover *all* the costs of running buses including, 'a reasonable return on capital employed'. Herbert Morrison spent his early years in poverty and he learnt the maxims of Mr Micawber.

Even in those days, however, it was recognized that not at all times nor in all places should the passenger cover the full cost of his particular trip. The principle of cross subsidization was understood, as it continues to be understood in almost every other service industry. The man who sends a letter from Land's End to John o'Groats is clearly cross subsidized by the man who sends a letter a distance of half a mile. The man who obtains his milk, his electricity and his refuse disposal by causing other people to come to him over long distances is also cross subsidized by others.

In the bus industry those travelling on lightly trafficked routes have traditionally been subsidized by those on busy routes, children by adults, the Sunday traveller by the weekday traveller. However, traditionally this has all been internal. The bus-using community, as a whole, paid its way.

The crunch comes when the passengers do not pay the operating costs of bus services. Cross subsidization must then be looked at critically and an operator will prefer to maintain services on well patronized, profitable routes, even when this means withdrawing cross subsidization from lesser used routes and services.

What happens then? Either the poor route bears its full costs or the poor route has its costs paid for by someone else.

A great deal of research has been carried out into what the market will bear in the way of fares increases (5.7). However this research is sometimes inconclusive because, where it is reliable, it supports common sense which tells us that it is indeed possible to over-price a bus service and thus to kill it simply on account of the price charged. With the niceties and the detail of the argument we need not be concerned. The principle remains obvious.

Finance from Other Sources

If total revenue from passengers is inadequate money must be found from elsewhere or the service must be discontinued. There is no other alternative and a great deal can be saved by recognizing this simple fact. What is important, and what is frequently insufficiently discussed, are the basic reasons and basic philosophy behind asking the community to finance bus services other than through direct payment for users.

Subsidies have become an increasing proportion of the bus operator's income, and the White Paper offers the prospect of this situation continuing, and perhaps increasing, in rural areas. In 1976, the NBC received money from grants etc. equal to some 15.7% of the revenue received direct from passengers in fares, compared with only 6.4% in 1969 (Table 5.2).

In many walks of life, this is already a well established principle. It is accepted that refuse-collection will be paid for in a different way from delivery of milk, even though some have virtually no refuse to be disposed of. It is also accepted by many, though not by all, that childless people should help to pay for the education of children they themselves have not conceived. The thinking behind this is that education is of value to the community generally and that the childless couple in old age will be financed by the people for whose education they have helped to pay, even though there is no blood relationship. This 'members one-of-another' philosophy extends into many other areas of life. We accept, subconsciously that we pay for many things we do not personally use or consume on the grounds that, thereby, we ultimately share, indirectly, in the benefits these payments lead to.

Accepting this general philosophy, how is it to be applied in practical terms to transport? As regards urban transport, the principle is not difficult to see applied. In Hamburg, for instance, and in other cities on the Continent, there is a clear policy that the passenger, at the time he boards the bus, should only contribute for half the cost of his mobility. The non passenger benefits in a number of ways. As a motorist he may benefit by having the passenger not using private transport and thus adding to congestion. He may benefit because the passenger, having achieved mobility, which he would not otherwise enjoy, is

TABLE 5.2   National Bus Company Revenue (Fares and Grants) 1969-1976

	1969 £m	1970 £m	1971 £m	1972 £m	1973 £m	1974 £m	1975 £m	1976 £m
Receipts from Passengers Fares	134.3	147.8	169.1	177.5	187.2	212.6	282.6	341.8
Receipts from Grants, etc								
Special grant	–	–	–	7.0	–	–	–	–
New Bus Grant*	2.0	1.8	3.6	5.1	6.6	7.3	9.0	14.6
Assistance for rural bus services*	–	–	1.1	1.1	1.6	2.8	1.3	–
Revenue Support grants**	–	–	–	–	–	–	6.5	21.6
Rail Replacement Services	–	–	0.3	0.1	–	–	–	–
Fuel duty – amount reimbursed	7.2	7.9	7.9	7.7	7.6	12.8	13.8	16.5
	9.2	9.7	12.9	21.0	15.8	22.9	30.6	52.7

* Under Transport Act 1968

** Under Local Government Act 1972

Source: Data derived from figures in National Bus Company Annual
Report 1976

able to give the non-passenger his service. This, after all, is the thinking behind levying a special tax on employers to help their employees get to work or, put more simply, the thinking behind works contract buses. Furthermore, we have the thinking expressed in a number of reports which set out the high cost in terms of infrastructure, of providing the same level of mobility by other means.

There are, therefore, three kinds of 'external benefit' that do not accrue directly to the traveller. Firstly, by using a less congesting form of transport community mobility is enhanced. Secondly, by using public transport, energy and environmental resources are not depleted so much. Thirdly, poorer people can get about and play a fuller and more satisfying part in the life of the community.

But how does this thinking apply when it comes to rural areas, especially since, in so many other parts of the world, it is disregarded? The United States, for example, is making great efforts in certain of its cities to break the thraldom and discomfort imposed by too much private transport. Little similar effort is being made in less densely populated areas.

It is possible, on a more limited front, to apply these arguments. For example, in the Goyt Valley in the Peak District National Park, it was shown that 16 people in a minibus will cause less problems in an area of outstanding natural beauty than 5 cars carrying the same number. Additionally, if rural areas are to be stripped of all public transport, the type of person who is encouraged to settle there has inevitably to be a car driver. The disabled and the old can therefore be condemned to urban life unless they have access to volunteer chauffeurs. As an example, it can be noted that council housing lists are often slightly shorter in areas where public transport does not exist. All have seen the evils of too great a concentration of one type of person in a given area. Jarrow in the 1930s was a less happy town than Warrington because it had a smaller variety of employ-ment. New towns sometimes suffer from too many young people just as the 'costa geriatrica' suffers from the reverse. Admittedly, the modern craze for social engineering must be practised with care but the basic fact should be recognized that lack of public transport in rural areas may tend to polarize them.

There is thus a case for someone other than the passenger contributing towards the finance of the rural bus. But we are more concerned with the practicalities than with the academic logic, and in practical terms in a time of financial stringency, government and tax payer alike are moving gently away from the thinking that non-passengers should contribute much more than half of the cost of running a rural bus, just as the bus operator is having thoughts on the degree of 'cross subsidization' he can sustain. The 50% maximum 'coat-hanger' was first made respectable by section 34 of the 1968 Transport Act which helped local authorities to contrbute to rural bus services without, incidentally, defining what a rural bus service was. This percentage could well increase under any legislation stemming from the 1977 Transport Policy White Paper (5.8).

But is 50% right? The most likely answer to this question is 'no'. Yet it has provided a pragmatic solution to the problem of rural bus financing for several years. How can this cost be justified and will there not be even more difficult questions to be answered if it were to be increased? For a start, there are many other competing claims for largesse of this order. For example, why should people be helped over transport and not helped in the provision of telephones or food or clothing or many other of the necessities of life? The arguments become deafening. There is the added problem that the traditional cost discipline is weakened. In the past it was possible to turn to bus manufacturers or to bus employees, demanding more money, and use that simple phrase 'it cannot be afforded'. If no limit is placed on public bounty this constraint is weakened.

A clear government (both central and local) philosophy is required, coupled with proper financial discipline. There are several possibilities; one is to separate out the truly social element of need by such methods as concessionary travel for special groups and then require the bus operator to plan his services in a way which carries most passengers within a pre-determined subsidy level. This leaves the operator and the market to sort out the 'best' service arrangements.

Another approach is for government to specify service 'needs' and to agree to pay for the costs of those not covered by fares. In rural areas, where the market is thin this may be the best solution, but, as yet, local government has not generally been sufficiently forthcoming as to what it believes the transport needs of rural areas to be. Also it has not always been forthcoming with the subsidy to ensure that these needs are met.

School Children

No discussion of the financing of the rural bus would be complete without some reference to school children who do form, sometimes, the largest and often the least tractable of transport problems in less densely populated areas. If universal education is to be provided, some transport must also be provided in order that the education can be received. The provision of transport becomes as much part of the total scene as the provision of books and stationery. It is an obligation which cannot be avoided. Yet the cost to a rural community of rounding up children scattered throughout the countryside on a mere 190 days a year, 5 days a week, for one journey in the morning and one in the afternoon, is rarely an economic proposition for anybody. The fact that government has for so long delayed any fresh response to this problem, points to its intractability. An uneven birthrate—uneven not only in total but also by counties—does not help in long term planning. The problem, probably does not begin as a transport problem, but one can understand the viewpoint of those operators who now refuse to supply duplicate buses in peak hours for scholars unless these are specifically paid for by local education authorities. This provides a classic example of a community service need which needs to be articulated in the prescription for rural bus services. In the follow up to the White Paper on Transport Policy the Government have suggested that counties draw up public transport plans. This should provide the opportunity for an expression of the bus services appropriate in rural areas and the basis on which local government sees their financing.

Methods of Finance

Almost as important as deciding how much should be financed and from where, is the business of ensuring that money passes from A to B. It is often a matter of astonishment to men, used to dealing in commodities, how complex money men make the transmission of their commodity from the donor to the recipient. What does have to be recognized is that the money business and the transport business have a longer time cycle than many are currently prepared to admit. A good deal of administration is still geared to a rural economy. Subconsciously, people think in yearly periods to coincide with the rhythm of the four seasons. Unfortunately a bus takes a long time to build once it has been ordered, and the necessary electricians, skilled fitters and general maintenance men take an even longer time to train. The bus itself is a flexible device, but the bus business cannot change direction quickly at six months notice and cannot be dependent on the outcome of a local election or a vote on next year's estimates before the total quantum that is needed is known. The theme song of lack of continuity is by now becoming hackneyed. It does need, though, to be understood why bus people are singing that song so often.

In addition to the matter of continuity, there are various other ways in which the smooth flow of money can be helped. Money, after all, is very like water. It has a cycle and is recycled in a fairly predictable manner. It does need, however, to be asked whether the cycle is as efficient and cost effective as it should be.

Buses handle a great deal of cash of which a large proportion is in coin form. Coins tend to move from passengers to buses, buses to banks, banks frequently to shops and from shops to individuals. It could be thought that in a reasonably self contained community such as, for example, the Isle of Wight during the winter months, the cycle would have been a smooth one. But it is not and the whole question of coin movement is something which could do with further study.

In addition to coins of the realm the bus industry handles a good deal of substitute money. Over £10 million worth of tokens are handled each year and with tokens coming in 2, 3 and 5p denominations, this means a good deal of actual token pieces. The problems of 2p tokens on a one-man bus can not be inconsiderable.

Quite apart from the logistics of cash and coin as a commodity is the matter of ensuring that money is available when required and is sensibly invested when it is not required. In a cash and often a seasonal business such as bus operation frequently is, the handling of the money flow can be important and the

71

investment of short term funds or the raising of short term loans can be a matter of nice judgement.

In this connection the leasing, renting or hiring of fixed assets has grown recently in importance. Some people tend to think of leasing as a high class form of tax avoidance. This may be so, where the lessor has tax profits and the lessee tax losses. But it is possible to overemphasize this aspect. An operator may lease if his judgement of the way interest rates are moving is different from the judgement of the lessor. If he, the lessee, thinks interest rates will rise, it can pay him to lease buses on a fixed rate contract rather than borrow the money from a bank which may have a rise and fall clause attached.

The point here is that the bus business is like other businesses in many respects. It needs planning, continuity, good industrial relations, cost control and skilled financial management if it is to give good value for money. Though these are not sufficient to solve the problem of financing bus services in rural areas they are all necessary if a satisfactory solution is to be achieved.

Conclusion

Four questions at the beginning of this chapter were listed. The first of them, namely how much bus transport is there, or ought there to be financed in less populated areas, is one basically for chapters other than this. The second question, the cost of providing transport, is one which is relatively simple to answer in broad outline. It is the detail which becomes complex. The basic cost of linking up men and materials to provide satisfactory and regular mobility for people in less densely populated areas is appreciable. Innovations can be tried and should be encouraged. These include encouraging the do-it-yourself element, relating supply more closely to demand, or combining the provision of transport with some other provision. They have to be recognized for what they are: as partial not universal answers.

To provide satisfactory bus transport in rural areas can be costly and the costs are unlikely to be met in full by the passenger at the time he boards the bus. Until recently this passenger has been cross subsidized by other passengers. The time has been reached when the other passenger is no longer so frequently able to cross subsidize and there is a danger of over charging the latter to the detriment of both. This being the case, we are searching for someone who is prepared to contribute and the search is not easy. The logic of getting someone other than, or additional to, the user does not need to be spelled out in detail and the consequences of moving the bus industry from the commercial to the partly social need to be fully appreciated. In less densely populated areas there is a limited case for getting the community to contribute. What is equally important is once it has been decided that the community shall pay, there should be some continuity of payment to enable longer term planning to be effective.

References

5.1 BRITISH RAILWAYS BOARD, *The Reshaping of British Railways*, (The Beeching Report), HMSO, 1963

5.2 Local Government Act 1972

5.3 DEPARTMENT OF THE ENVIRONMENT, *Local Transport Grants, Circular 104/73*, HMSO, 1973

5.4 *Transport Policy*, (CMND 6836), HMSO, 1977

5.5 NBC, *National Bus Company Annual Report 1976*, 1977

5.6 *HANSARD 1929*, ref. London Transport Bill

5.7 'Symposium on Public Transport Fare Structures: Papers and Discussion', *TRRL Supplementary Report 37 UC*, 1974

5.8 *Transport Policy, op. cit.*

CHAPTER SIX

Transport in the County Budget

K.R. Hounsome

The new counties created in England and Wales in 1974, under the Local Government Act 1972, were given powers in that Act to coordinate public passenger transport in their areas. The Act introduced new arrangements for financing local transport services based on the annual allocation by the government of the Transport Supplementary Grant. To qualify for this each county is required to prepare an annual Transport Policy and Programme (TPP) giving details of both highways and public transport proposals (6.1). This chapter which contains a case study of North Yorkshire, examines the place of transport in the county budget. North Yorkshire provides an excellent basis for this case study as it contains a high road mileage and a wide variety of rural areas with differing needs for public transport operations.

The first sections of this chapter describe in some detail the background to the preparation of the county transportation budget at the present time. The government's planning of public expenditure forms part of this background and is described in some detail, both because of its growing importance at a time of financial difficulty and because of the author's former involvement as financial advisor for transportation finance to the Association of County Councils. This should be of interest to those engaged in this important local government service. The later sections of the chapter take the reader from the national scene back to the local problems of North Yorkshire.

North Yorkshire is the largest of the new counties in area. It stretches over 3200 sq. miles (8300 km²), across from the east coast nearly to the west. There are 5368 miles (8638 km) of county roads for the County Council to maintain and agency functions are exercised over 263 miles (424 km) of motorways and trunk roads. The County Council itself grants agency powers for highways to the York City Council and for part of their areas to the Harrogate and Scarborough Borough Councils.

Responsibility for transportation at committee level rests with the Highways and Transportation Committee, which itself is helped by four Area Advisory Committees incorporating, for areas not covered by agency agreements, representatives of district councils. In addition, a small Passenger Transport Sub-Committee considers the granting of bus subsidies and related matters. A Joint Sub-Committee also exists, meeting irregularly to coordinate matters of mutual concern to the Highways and Transportation Committee, the Planning Committee and the two National Parks Committees. The control over the County Council's finances is exercised by the Policy and Resources Committee, mainly through its Finance Sub-Committee.

A Local Authority Budget

An essential part of an independent, democratically elected system of local government is the freedom of the elected members of the local authority to determine both the level and the make-up of its expenditure. The main instrument of its decision making in this field is its annual budget. This is needed each year by an authority in order to fix its rate which, for the county council, is in the form of a precept upon its district councils. These in their turn add an amount needed for their own requirements and then levy a total rate on the assessed annual value of each property in its area. The annual budget usually also incorporates the capital expenditure programme of the authority. The current thinking in local government is increasingly to regard the whole document as part of the longer-term corporate planning of the authority.

Freedom to fix its own budget is, however, circumscribed in a number of ways. First, there are the legal restraints associated with borrowing, and the payment of government grant. Capital expenditure, if it is to be financed by borrowing, needs a loan sanction. This sanction must be granted specifically by a government department if it is regarded as a 'key sector' service, be met from the county's 'locally determined' allocation covering both the needs of the county council and the districts, or be covered by a 'general consent' as in the purchase of land. In transportation at the present time a 'key sector' allocation is granted on the basis of the TPP submission for projects estimated to cost over half a million pounds. For the minority of services (principally for a county's police) still financed by a specific grant calculated at a percentage of expenditure, prior approval is required of a government department for many new items of expenditure.

Secondly, local authorities are given a number of mandatory duties by Parliament (for example, to provide education for the children resident in their areas) and would be liable by law if they neglected them. Further consideration of the mandatory services, however, would indicate that in most cases the local authority has considerable freedom in determining the standard at which a service is provided (for example, in education the pupil/teacher ratio). Conversely, by the doctrine of *ultra vires*, expenditure must be either specifically authorized or reasonably implied from its statutory powers.

Thirdly, a local authority preparing for each new financial year finds that a large part of its budget is committed already by the cost of the staff it employs, the building which it uses and by the cost of servicing its past loan debt. This undoubted fact however, has encouraged local authorities to concentrate their attention overmuch on the 'growth' items in their budgets to the exclusion of the much greater committed figures where, albeit difficult, policy decisions might lead to the release of substantial resources for better use elsewhere.

Lastly, its freedom of action is, in practice, limited by the wishes of the government in carrying out its economic policy. Local government's expenditure on current account in 1976/77 is expected to total £10 717 million and a further £2889 million on capital account. It accounts for 26% of the total public expenditure, which in itself is about 52% of the nation's total income. The days are long past, therefore, when a government could ignore the budgets of local authorities in its management of the nation's economy. The powers already described are a part of its armoury of compulsion. However, in addition, the government has considerable powers of persuasion, partly by constant exhortation of local authorities to follow its wishes, and partly by use of its Rate Support Grant which finances just under two-thirds of the expenditure of local government. Furthermore, and uniquely for a major local government service, the Department of the Environment hitherto, and now the recreated Department of Transport, has a weapon of persuasion of great, but still of limited, force in its distribution of the Transport Supplementary Grant based on its examination of each county's TPP.

The exhortations, expressed in speech and circular, have of course in recent years sought to restrain expenditure, but the various spokesmen of government have not always spoken with the same voice. Examples could be quoted of pressure for further expenditure from parts of Whitehall when local government has been encouraged to economize. However, there are signs that the economic crisis, and perhaps the opportunity for local government leaders to make their views known regularly through the new Local Government Finance Council, have led to a much needed improvement. While the wishes of government are listened to by local government, the response, inevitably, varies from one authority to another. At the present time the need for economy corresponds with the wishes both of many local authority members, and perhaps just as important, of the electors upon whose votes they depend. More thoughtful members realize, also, that the price of preserving local government freedoms and of controlling their own budgets may well mean the readiness of local authorities to respond to the dictates of the government's economic policy.

The Public Expenditure Survey and the Rate Support Grant

The government's wishes are also given expression in the periodical Survey of Public Expenditure; the most recent one, published in February 1977, covers the five financial years up to 31 March 1981. The summary of the government's wishes covers the whole of the public sector but recognizes that, while detailed figures are given for each local government service, local authorities are able (subject to the constraints already mentioned) to determine their own policies. The figures for local government services given for the second year of each Survey (1977/8 in the 1977 publication) reflect the Rate Support Grant settlement for that year. They differ in one important respect, in that capital expenditure is included in the Survey and, therefore, to avoid double counting, local authority loan charges are omitted.

It is the Rate Support Grant Settlement which gives real teeth to the government's wishes for local government expenditure. By its determination of the total of relevant expenditure upon which the grant is based, the government gives precise expression to the amount of local government expenditure on current account that it wishes to be incurred. The block grant principle, by which it distributes the largest part of its grant to metropolitan districts and non-metropolitan counties (called the 'needs' element) ensures that the effect of each pound incurred or saved is felt wholly by the local authority itself. With the high rate of grant represented by the needs grant, a powerful gearing effect is felt. By this is meant that any growth in expenditure significantly above or below that upon which the grant is based will lead to a proportionately larger increase or reduction in the local rate.

The government's determination of the relevant expenditure upon which the Rate Support Grant is based follows discussions over several months each year with representatives of the local authority associations. At one time these were negotiations in the true sense, but over the past two years the process has concerned itself with spelling out in detail the effect of a predetermined amount of grant announced in advance by the government. The most achieved by the local government representatives in the course of long discussions has been a relatively small addition of extra money released by the government from other votes and the transfer of money from capital programmes into the current expenditure recognized for the Rate Support Grant.

The detailed calculation of the figures each year is entrusted to six expenditure sub-groups composed of civil servants and local authority representatives drawn from treasurers' offices at the number two or number three level. One of these sub-groups is for transportation. At a later stage the main points thrown up by the sub-groups are argued out with the civil servants by the treasurers and other service advisors to the associations, with the major points left unsettled being referred upwards to the local authority leaders meeting ministers in the Consultative Council.

When the 1976 Public Expenditure Survey was published the local authority associations again, in the Consultative Council, made the point that it was difficult for the local authorities to accept the implications of the detailed figures given for local government services when they had played no part in the preparation of the survey. In response to this argument the government decided that the same machinery established for the Rate Support Grant should be used to discuss the figures built into the Public Expenditure Survey. The timetable for this has meant that the sub-groups now have to start their work in May instead of September. Linked to the work of the sub-groups there is now for each of them a parallel consideration of the policy implications of the figures by what is now a formally constituted steering group of civil servants, treasurers and service advisors.

The local authority involvement for the first time in the Public Expenditure Steering Committee (PESC) exercise, through the sub-group and steering-group, took place against the background of both Circular 45/76 (Local Authority Current Expenditure 1976/77) (6.2) and of the reductions of public expenditure then under consideration by the government and eventually announced on 22 July 1976. Circular 45/76 drew attention to the potential 'overspending' by local authorities on current account in 1976/77 of about £417 million compared with that determined by the government in the Rate Support Grant settlement for that year. The significance of this for this chapter is that a notable part of the 'overspending', in fact about £132 million, appeared to come from local transport. Of this £73 million appeared to arise on revenue support of buses, £21 million on concessionary fares and £38 million on highway maintenance. The figures for the first two items seemed realistic, the potential 'overspending' arising mainly in the metropolitan areas. The third possible 'overspending', that on highway maintenance, was questioned by the local authority members of the sub-group who, using the statistics prepared jointly by the County Treasurers' and County Surveyors' Societies, thought that the figure was inflated; later it was established that the sub-group was probably right. Further estimates based on examination of spending plans for 1976/77 given in the submission in July 1976 of the 1977/78 TPPs indicated a potential overall 'overspending' not of £132 million but of only £50 million on current account, and even this was likely to be wholly or partly offset by savings on capital schemes. Of current expenditure, revenue support for buses and the London Underground, and on concessionary fares, was still likely to exceed substantially the government's PESC estimate by £68 million, but the TPPs figures showed not an 'overspending' but a potential saving on highway maintenance.

The sub-group's and steering group's work is concerned, however, mainly with the future—in particular their attention is concentrated on the year immediately ensuing. It is that year, of course, which is vitally important for the PESC planning as it forms the basis of the Rate Support Grant for that year.

TABLE 6.1 Changes in the Government's Plan for Local Transport Expenditure in 1977/78

	Command* 6393	Working Group proposals for distribution of Command 6393 amended	Settlement	Settlement Repriced
	(1)	(2)	(3)	(4)
	£million	£million	£million	£million
CURRENT EXPENDITURE				
Roads Maintenance	372.5	371.0	369.1	422.3
Car Parks – net	– 16.1	– 7.2	– 7.2	– 7.2
Concessionary Fares	51.2	78.3	78.3	99.4
Administration	153.1	150.0	150.0	171.6
Revenue Support	109.7	143.3	156.8	175.1
Total Current	670.4	735.4	747.0	861.2
CAPITAL				
Roads and Lighting	262.6	191.1	164.3	169.4
Car Parks	26.2	8.3	8.3	9.2
Public Transport	102.6	100.0	100.0	114.4
Total Capital	391.4	299.4	272.6	293.0
TOTAL CAPITAL AND CURRENT	1,061.8	1,034.8	1,019.6	1,154.2

Note

1. The figures in columns (1), (2) and (3) are based on November 1975 prices, and those in column (4) on prices at November 1976.
2. The capital figures in column (3) have been adjusted by the reduction of £26.8m on roads and lighting requested by the Chancellor in December 1976.

* Public Expenditure to 1979/80 (Command 6393) HMSO.

Their work is best summarized by an examination of the figures in Table 6.1. The Public Expenditure Survey figures do not, of course bind local authorities, but they do represent government policy and local authorities can therefore expect pressure to be exerted for at least a broad compliance with the figures.

A feature of local authority transport finance in recent years has been the efforts by the government to reduce the substantial amount being paid for revenue support of buses by the Greater London Council and the metropolitan counties. The 1976/77 RSG settlement expected for all counties a figure of £112 million at November 1975 prices, but the latest evidence available in the autumn, and revealed by the submission of the 1977/78 TPPs, showed a likely figure of £175 million for 1977. For 1977/78, Command 6393 planned a further reduction to £87 million, but the TPPs showed that local authorities intended to spend £174 million. The local authority representatives considered that a figure of £120 million was the lowest that could be expected in 1977/78 and that even this would require substantial further economies, particularly in some metropolitan areas. It would also require a major policy change by some of the metropolitan counties and the government's partially successful effort to achieve this led to the final figure for 1977/78 of £133 million. Time will tell whether it is achieved.

As to concessionary fares, this item of expenditure was transferred in the National Budget from the Department of Health and Social Security to local transport for the first time in Command 6393. With it local transport inherited a low estimate by the government of the current cost, and a recent joint working party of government and local authority representatives ascertained that the cost for 1976/77 was running at £77 million and that this, therefore, should form the basis of future estimates.

Alarm was expressed, too, at the government's figures for highway mainte-nance and for car parking. It was clear to the local authority officers that it was unrealistic of the government to expect local authorities to follow the very harsh policies that its figure implied. A preliminary view of the reasonable level of highway maintenance that could be expected (£400 million at 1975 prices) was formed with the help of the timely survey carried out by the County Surveyors' Society that showed that in many counties earlier cuts made in highway maintenance expenditure has reduced the standard of the roads to a condition where substantial further cuts would be considered self-defeating in the longer term. Later in the summer the TPPs showed that the figure of £400 million was untenable; authorities, perhaps with some misgivings, it seems were then planning to spend next year close to the Command 6393 figure of £371 million. For car parking the government's policy of expecting a doubling of the income from charges by 1978/79 was considered as quite unobtainable and lacking in realism by its failure to distinguish the variety of circumstances under which a local authority's car parking policy are formed.

expenditure in the eyes of the present government and, perhaps, the relative weakness of the special pressure groups (compared, for example, with the teachers) to influence government expenditure decisions.

TABLE 6.2 Local Authority Expenditure in England and Wales

	1976/77 £million	1977/78 £million	1978/79 £million	1979/80 £million
Roads and Transport (which includes the	1,053	938	842	838
following public	(232)	(205)	(176)	(171)
transport expenditure)	22%	22%	21%	20%
Agriculture, Fisheries and Forestry		1	1	1
Trade, Industry and Employment	36	34	35	36
Housing	2,057	2,035	2,071	2,089
Other Environmental Services	1,115	1,127	1,084	1,068
Law, Order and Protective Services	972	971	963	964
Education and Libraries, Science and Arts	4,665	4,618	4,563	4,538
Health and Personal Social Services	711	718	731	745
Other Public Services	62	61	61	61
	10,671	10,503	10,351	10,340

Basic Source 'Public Expenditure to 1979/80' Command 6393, HMSO—1975 Survey prices

With all these factors in mind it is perhaps of interest to summarize by committee the estimated net expenditure, met from rates, RSG, and TSG, on current account of North Yorkshire County Council proposed for 1977/78. Table 6.3 also shows the reduction of estimated net expenditure on other than loan charges and capital expenditure financed from revenue in 'real' terms compared with the previous year.

In arriving at the above figures the County's expenditure planning had to be modified during the last few weeks of the budget process. At the end of November the Rate Support Grant settlement was announced (it included a substantial overall reduction in government grant aid to local government and for North Yorkshire a loss in 1977/78 as in earlier years of a substantial sum due to changes in the distribution formula of the needs part of the grant). This led

TABLE 6.3 North Yorkshire County Council Estimated
Net Expenditure 1977/8

Committee	Net current expenditure	Reduction in expenditure on other than loan charges and capital expenditure financed from revenue compared with 1976/77
	£000	£000
Agricultural	32.1	5.0–
Education	74,338.1	293.2–
Highways and Transportation*	15,352.6	834.0–
Library, Archives and Museums	2,274.6	48.0–
North York Moors National Park	118.8	1.2–
Planning	813.8	12.3–
Police	5,645.1	69.9–
Policy and Resources		
– Committee Expenditure	1,587.8	38.8–
– Contingency Sum	7,920.0	–
Public Protection	3,285.9	120.1–
Social Services	10,069.8	166.3+
Yorkshire Dales National Park	123.9	3.4+
TOTAL	121,562.5	1,252.8–

* Included in this heading is expenditure on waste disposal which is an additional responsibility of the Highways and Transportation Committee.

the Finance Sub-Committee to seek further reductions in expenditure to mitigate what otherwise would be a 25% increase in rates. In the members' view such an increase was politically unacceptable particularly in a year of county council elections. The Highways and Transportation Committee was asked to make its contribution by finding further savings of £633 000 from its planned expenditure which had already been reduced to meet earlier guidelines. This amount was part of further savings of £3.3m sought from all committees in an effort to reduce the county rate from a possible 65p to 61p. At this lower level the amount still represents a 17% increase above the 52p level in 1976/77.

The TPP and the Budget

Before moving on to consider the detailed make-up of North Yorkshire County Council transportation budget, framed by the Highways and Transportation Committee within the Policy and Resources Committee guidelines described, it is appropriate to consider first the part that the TPP submitted to the Department of the Environment in July each year plays. Some may be surprised that it has not formed a more prominent part of this chapter. The TPP, it must be remembered, is not a statutory document. Its formal purpose is merely to enable the government each year to distribute its Transport Supplementary Grant, with an additional function, as already explained, of forming the basis of the allocation of key sector loan sanction. To put it crudely, the TPP is, in effect, a bid for grant and loan sanction.

This blunt treasurers' view of the TPP is no doubt heresy to those who spend a great deal of their time in the preparation of the document, and to those who lead the way in the exotic art of corporate planning. To them a TPP should fit in precisely to not only the long term transportation planning of a local authority, but its financial policy as well. Two things militate against this most desirable objective. First, there is, in effect, a chicken and egg situation in the TPP submission; members are entitled to say 'tell us the amount of the TSG which we will receive and we will tell you how much we will spend'. Secondly, and more importantly, is the time scale and the timing of the document. In the rapidly changing financial scene for local authorities it is difficult for them to look forward to one financial year, let alone five. Some authorities may, in fact, issue to their Transportation Committee the budget guidelines in the preceding spring, which is early enough to form the cost basis of the TPP. Most county councils find this too early and the TPP has therefore to be prepared without formal guidance in advance from the Policy and Resources Committee. In practice however, informal help is often given by the County Treasurer to the County Surveyor and his staff as to the broad financial basis on which the TPP should be produced to be acceptable to the Policy and Resources Committee.

This is not to say the TPP is submitted without a financial appraisal. Much the reverse. After its approval by the Transportation Committee the TPP is translated into terms of revenue growth rates for each year of its duration. This

85

is done by the introduction of loan charges (in accordance with the established financing policy of the county council) and administration, and by the elimination of district council expenditure. The Finance Sub-Committee of the Policy and Resources Committee is then asked to consider whether the financial effect thus calculated is acceptable, or at least is not too far away from the likely expenditure to be contemplated in the coming budget.

Of the three TPPs submitted so far, all but the first were judged by the Finance Sub-Committee to be a realistic document to submit to the Department of the Environment. The exception led to a demand for a reduction fixed by the Finance Sub-Committee and settled in detail by a Special Sub-Committee of the Highways and Transportation Committee.

The TPP is also the first indication that the Finance Sub-Committee is likely to have of a large scheme contemplated at the end of the TPP period by the Highways and Transportation Committee. The evaluation process which has been referred to enables the Finance Sub-Committee to give at least a cautious preliminary view as to whether the particular scheme is likely to be acceptable on financial grounds.

The extent to which the submitted TPP and the level of 'accepted' expenditure subsequently agreed by the Department of Transport are permitted to influence a county council's transportation budget must vary a great deal from one authority to another. In these harsh times the level of transportation spending, if not its make-up, cannot be divorced from the important budget and rate levying policies of the County Council. These are usually formulated some time after the submission of the TPP but have gone a long way towards the final determination before the accepted expenditure and amount of TSG is notified in December. As a matter of principle, too, many members of local authorities would not sacrifice lightly their freedom in this important area. In the same way, many view with some distaste the practice of the Department of Transport to itemize, in its notification of a county's TSG, the amount allowed in the total of accepted expenditure for particular items. In the County's 1976/77 notification the amounts for revenue support and highway maintenance were specifically mentioned and the more sensitive of us see this as a tendency to itemize the TSG and to depart from its block grant concept.

Reference should perhaps now be made to the relationship of the TPP to the Structure Plan. This reference, for North Yorkshire, can only be brief because the Structure Plan of the County is still in the course of preparation. Clearly, however, the TPP of any county must fit into the broad transportation strategy outlined in the Structure Plan and it is to be expected that both the County Planning Officer and, in our case, the Joint Highways Planning Sub-Committee, to whom the TPP is submitted each year, will pay special attention to this.

The Transportation Budget

As has been explained, the cost of the first year covered by the TPP document as submitted in any year could well, in North Yorkshire, prove to be at least marginally different from what eventually appears in the transportation budget. There is no doubt, however, that the statement of policies which it contains is a strong influence on the make-up of the transportation budget. Indeed, it would be strange if it were not so. The County Surveyor, in deciding the precise mixture of expenditure which he proposes to the Highways and

TABLE 6.4   North Yorkshire County Council Transportation Budget 1977/78

Revenue Expenditure	Expenditure	Income	Net Expenditure to be met from County Rates and Grants	
	£000	£000	£000	%
Administration	1,976.3	–	1,976.3	14
Maintenance of County Roads	10,052.1	497.1	9,555.0	67
Improvements of County Roads	1,995.6	–	1,995.6	14
Maintenance of Motorways and Trunk Roads	2,008.2	2,008.2	–	
Improvements of Motorways and Trunk Roads	2,477.9	2,477.9	–	
Revenue Support to Bus Operators	730.0	–	730.0	5
	19,240.1	4,983.2	14,256.9	100

Capital Expenditure (Gross)	£
Highway Improvement	2,007.7
Depots and Offices	51.2
Plant and Vehicles	393.8
	2,452.7

Note: Prices as at November 1976

Transportation Committee in the draft estimates, and based of course on the budget guidelines laid down by the Policy and Resources Committee, is in his turn guided considerably by the approved policies of the County Council as contained in the TPP. However, references may be made to the breakdown of the 1977/78 transportation budget for North Yorkshire under main heads given in Table 6.4.

Administration

Administration, estimated to cost £2 305 500 in total, covers three main heads—the County Surveyor's Department including the four area offices (£1 752 300), the apportioned cost of the County Treasurer's, Clerk's and County Valuers Departments (£307 100) and the payment for administration to the three agent authorities (£246 100). This cost is reduced by the recharge made to the waste disposal account and by the recharge to the Department of Transport for administration of the trunk road agency works.

Highway maintenance

Expenditure on highway maintenance takes up about two-thirds of the North Yorkshire Transportation budget and, therefore, quite naturally it has figured prominently in the budget discussions of the County Council in recent years. It affords a local authority room to manoeuvre to a much larger extent than does expenditure on many other services. How much depends on how its work is carried out. Those authorities like North Yorkshire who traditionally have employed large direct labour forces find, if redundancies are to be avoided, that there is a strict limit to the speed at which expenditure can be reduced, even if it were wise to do so. Whether it is wise to inflict a further substantial cut on highway maintenance expenditure in 1977/78 after the reductions of earlier years was for North Yorkshire, like others, a difficult decision. It was only with some misgivings, particularly after studying the report of the County Surveyor, that members decided that if the government's wishes for total local government spending were to be adhered to in North Yorkshire, and given the problems associated with making further cuts in other services, the cut of about 6% must be incorporated in the block saving asked of the Highways and Transportation Committee and subsequently incorporated, with only a minor adjustment, in their estimates. An even greater reduction, as part of the eleventh hour effort to restrain a large rate increase, only served to aggravate the painful decision facing members. Here it is appropriate to mention the Minister of Transport's own admission that the cut demanded was a shot in the dark in the absence of more detailed knowledge of the state of local authority roads. This gap the Department hopes to fill from the regular monitoring, based on a sample survey for each county, which its Standing Committee on Highways Maintenance has recently introduced.

Winter maintenance is an important subject in the North Yorkshire budget, although a succession of mild winters has made some people forget what a large bill can be incurred in a bad year. Expenditure under this head plays havoc with budgetary control and with the planning of other maintenance work. It is pleasing, therefore, that the new county followed the North Riding practice of budgeting for an average sum each year (£744 000 in 1977/78) on the understanding that savings and overspendings fall on the County Council's working balance. This means that the County Surveyor can plan his maintenance programme without the necessity to keep money on one side in case the winter is severe. The mild winters which we have experienced have ensured, however, that a 'profit' each year has accrued to the County Council since this commonsense approach was introduced.

Agent authorities

In North Yorkshire three district councils, York, Harrogate and Scarborough, are agent authorities, the last two only in respect of the urban parts of their districts. The agreement provides for the district to carry out highway maintenance work and improvements estimated to cost up to £100 000. Their engineers sit with the County's officers in the steering group of officers supervising the production of the TPP. The County's budget procedure provides for the submission of expenditure requests by the three agent authorities, the assessment, in the first instance by the County Surveyor, of the relative priorities of these schemes compared with the others and, of course, regular liaison with them as the budget process proceeds to its conclusion. The district councils, however, are given a percentage allowance for administration, thus avoiding a detailed examination of their claims for reimbursement.

Trunk road improvements and maintenance

The County Council itself, of course, is the agent of the Department of Transport for certain trunk road improvements and maintenance works. The expenditure and reimbursement are included in the County Council's budget and its significance to the financial planning of the County Council is perhaps two-fold. First, the reimbursement of administration expenses under the Department's scale affects directly the rate-borne expenditure of the Highways and Transportation Committee. Second is the effect of the expenditure on the direct labour force and, therefore, the minimum size of the total highways budget if redundancies are to be avoided.

Revenue support of buses

The growing effect of this item on the budget of a rural county is shown by the following figures:

1974/75	£120 000
1975/76	£432 000
1976/77 (revised estimate)	£750 000
1977/78 (final estimate)	£730 000

Nevertheless, the provision for 1977/78 represents only 5.1% of the transportation current expenditure budget. It is of interest that the average for all non-metropolitan counties in 1976/77 was 7.5%. For the GLC it was 58.8% and for the other metropolitan counties 17.4%. In terms of payments per 1000 population the 1976/77 figures are as follows:

North Yorkshire	£1147.7
Average non-metropolitan counties	£1177.6
Greater London Council	£10 575.5
Average for metropolitan counties	£3393.7

What of the future? Predictions are foolish, but hopefully the total of subsidies at constant cost and prices can be contained somewhere near the 1977/78 total. The containment, if it comes off, will be due in no small measure to the county council's policy since its formation of pressing for fare increases in line with inflation. Quickly on reorganization the County Council also adopted the Department of the Environment yardstick for its former rural bus grant, thus requiring that income from fares should normally amount to at least 50% of the expenditure (including apportioned overheads) on routes for which subsidy is claimed. At the same time a detailed study of bus services in each area of the county is being undertaken by the County Surveyor's staff in consultation with the district council concerned. This has now been completed in three areas of the County and is proving a useful means of achieving a rationalization of services and with it some financial saving. Experimental services have also been instituted and, naturally, liaison with the Education Department, whose bill for school transport amounts to about £1.5 million per annum, is recognized as very important. The County, too, is one of two English counties selected for the experimental relaxation of licensing requirements.

Negotiations with the bus companies over their subsidies have been tough but, hopefully, fairly conducted. Inevitably, the financial management of the various companies varies a great deal and the government's Transportation Consultative Document led us to consider whether or not an injection of county council members into the NBC companies would be a good step. It may be that bus services in the more rural parts of the County are more and more of the nature of social services and less an exercise in the coordination of transportation. Incidentally, concessionary fares which, as we have seen, are of growing financial importance, are paid for by only 12 of the 47 non-metropolitan counties. In North Yorkshire, like the remainder, they are left to the district councils and seven of the eight have schemes. It is worthy of note, too, that the non-metropolitan counties and their districts are paying only £4.4 per head of population of pensionable age in concessionary fares in 1976/77, compared with £18.2 in the metropolitan areas and £14.2 in London. Perhaps this is one more example of a higher standard of service in urban areas.

The Allocation of the Transport Supplementary Grant

One interesting little job for the County Treasurer in December each year is the treatment of the TSG in his budget. The Department of Transport decides this to some extent by its appropriation of part of the TSG to reduce the key sector loan sanctions necessary to carry out projects estimated to cost over half a million pounds. In other words, TSG must, to this extent, be credited to capital and not to revenue account. Other than this it is up to the authority and the question is, how much more should be credited to capital account to reduce borrowing and how much should be credited to revenue account to relieve rate-borne expenditure. In furtherance of the County's policy of financing as much capital expenditure as possible without recourse to borrowing, North Yorkshire's policy has been to credit TSG equal to 70% of all capital expenditure which would otherwise have been met from borrowing. The 1977/78 TSG is to be £4.6 million and £0.6 million is expected to be used in this way, leaving £4 million to be credited to the revenue account.

Budgetary Control

The County Council's budget, including of course that for transportation, receives the approval of the county council in February each year. Approval, however, is not the end of the matter. It then becomes a very live document for the day-to-day control of its expenditure throughout the year. The County Council's standing orders, however, give all committees a generous degree of what is termed 'virement' (i.e. the power to switch from one budget head to another). Up to £24 000 of the virement is allowed to each committee of the county council but traditionally the Highways expenditure of the Transportation Committee has been dealt with even more generously. It has been recognized that, because of the difficulty in timing schemes due principally to delay in land purchase, flexibility should be given to the Highways and Transportation Committee to vary expenditure between maintenance and

91

improvements, and between one improvement and another, provided the budgeted rate-borne expenditure for the year is not exceeded.

A new feature of local government finance, introduced by the government in 1976/77, is its application of its policy of cash limits to the Rate Support Grant and the Transport Supplementary Grant. Under this policy the usual increase during the course of each year to its grants to help meet inflation is to be limited to a predetermined percentage. The implication for local government is clear and could be painful if the government's estimate of inflation goes seriously astray. Immediate cuts in expenditure would then be needed if financial problems are to be avoided. In fact, the first experience of this took place in North Yorkshire in 1976/77. The practice is for the County Surveyor to submit a request for a supplementary estimate to the June meeting each year, reporting on cost increases since the budget was prepared the previous autumn. In 1976/77 this report showed that about £1.3 million was needed to compensate for cost increases on current account, principally for the rise in prices of materials used in highway maintenance. The Finance Sub-Committee recommendation, accepted by the Policy and Resources Committee, was that if the County Council's contingency sum set aside to meet inflation was to be safeguarded, £1 million was all that could be safely granted. Thus, sadly, and it could happen again in 1977/78, the bad news for the transportation service in North Yorkshire does not end with the approval of its budget.

References

6.1 Local Transport Grants, *Department of the Environment Circular 104/73*, HMSO, 1973
6.2 Local Authority Current Expenditure 1976/77, *Department of the Environment Circular 45/76*, HMSO, 1976
6.3 Public Expenditure to 1979/80, *Command 6393*, HMSO, 1976

PART TWO DISCUSSION
Rural Transport Policy and Finance
Chairman: R.L.W. Moon

E.P. HINKLEY (West Sussex County Surveyors' Department)

We appear to be faced with an Oxfordshire versus Bedfordshire approach. The Oxfordshire theory is likeable, but it is doubtful whether it will work in practice for reasons that have been touched on by Mr. Blowers. There is an element of selfishness in each of us and an extremely narrow view will tend to emerge at parish level. People who get involved in parish council work are usually involved in a number of other things such as the Women's Institute, church activities, youth clubs, local pressure groups etc. This requires much enthusiasm and perserverance and it is essential to have sustained interest to produce a local bus service. Draft minimum standards of service put forward in West Sussex are partially subjective but use some 1971 Census data on population and non-car ownership and these have been put to members for them to decide whether they form a reasonable basis for desk-top exercise. Only those services that make a loss are modified. Those that are profit making are left alone—at least to start with. On other services, levels of service are reduced until they reach break-even point or the threshold of the draft minimum standard that members have thought reasonable for the purpose of this exercise. If they become profit making before they reach the threshold, they are left at that level. Other than that, services will reduce to the basic threshold and at that point the county council will intervene with a subsidy to maintain the draft minimum standard level. At the end of the exercise which is being carried out with the help of the National Bus Company (NBC) subsidiaries and private operators, a network and level of subsidy will be decided on. It will then be open to the members to decide whether they can afford more or less and thus either raise or lower the standards accordingly. Both urban and rural standards have been prepared.

It seems inevitable, whether the Oxford or Bedford type of approach is followed, that there will have to be reductions in levels of service in urban and rural areas. There have to be changes and although the NBC may be *willing* to accept change, it is debatable whether they are *able* to accept it. From Mr. Neely it seems that there was a chance that they would change as he recognizes that mobility in rural areas is best provided by pedestrians, cyclists and motorists. However, later he failed to grasp the nettle of service reductions. Of course there is going to have to be some subsidy, but subsidy and levels of service must be related. I would like to ask Mr. Neely whether he too believes that there are going to be some reductions in this field. If he does not believe that, then what NBC evidence is there to support an alternative view?

A.D.W. SMITH (County Surveyor, Kent)

I agree with Mr. Blowers that these investigations are good, but, as Mr. Neely stated it does mean a great deal of staff time and now that politicians have cut down our staff levels it makes it very difficult. When going round on the Kent Structure Plan participation exercise, we asked the question 'What do you consider is the minimum level of service?' but nobody seemed to know. In the end we wrote our own idea of a level of service into the Structure Plan. This was very low indeed but to implement it would have meant doubling the present subsidy. Quite recently urban services were paying their way and it was only rural services that had to be subsidized. Now the reverse is true.

Many troubles could be due to the accounting system. Mr. Neely was very much to the point when he suggested that what the National Bus Company pay in rates returns to it in subsidies. In Kent, the NBC subsidiaries pay to the government roughly the same amount in interest and loan charges as the county council pay them in subsidies. The NBC pays the interest to the government, the government gives 70% in Transport Supplementary Grant to the county council and the county council hands it back to the NBC. The system seems crazy when with a stroke of the pen all this could be eliminated—it is just a paper transaction.

M. BUCHANAN (Colin Buchanan & Partners)

It may be true in Holland, where the subsidy levels appear very alarming, that the bus industry is financially reliant on the government. However, in the UK the money is undoubtedly with the passengers. Therefore the planning of routes and the question of subsidy should really start with the bus passengers and the bus operator and not with central government. Most of the journeys the bus passenger makes are very short and also, with rural passengers, many journeys are into towns. This suggests that the planning and subsidy question really needs to be tackled on a town/bus company/district basis rather than on a central government or possibly even a county council basis. In principle, subsidy may not be a bad thing but there does not seem much reason for some of the current cross subsidies. Ninety per cent of the population will prefer an increase in fares rather than an increase in rates—they do not really trust politicians to subsidize them effectively and would rather pay and have the money themselves in their pockets.

Subsidies will undoubtedly be justified by local authorities in two circumstances: in congested urban areas, whre it is very difficult to run a bus service because of the congestion, and also where there appear to be benefits to be gained from subsidizing buses rather than making a capital investment such as obtained in Stevenage. However, in that particular case, it would be interesting to see an updated version of the calculations to see the effect of the enormous inflation of bus costs. What will happen to bus services if this kind of subsidy is applied? The answer would probably be that many more tailor-made local convenience services running once a week on market days to a particular place would be seen. Some trimming of operations by the big companies would occur. The bus companies on the whole would emerge from the exercise leaner and healthier and there would probably be a big move against cross subsidy between services. For example, it is certainly true in Midland Red's area, where my organization as consultants to the company are engaged in a survey of passenger requirements, that the rural services are subsidizing the town services and the inter-urban services are subsidizing both. More private operators may be seen as well as hopefully lower fares because it is the fare levels that people dislike most about the bus service at present. Then finally there is a need to consider what will happen if services are not adjusted in this way. If the present pattern of services is retained there are bound to be fewer passengers over the years as car ownership goes up and demand declines; so there will be an inevitable tendency to try and pay for the same services by increasing the fares in real terms which will lead to even fewer passengers. Thus, a position may be reached in the long-term where, by cutting and adjusting services, more passengers are actually carried by being able to reduce the fares.

G.D. NEELY (National Bus Company)

Mr. Hinkley and Mr. Smith have demonstrated forcefully the difficulty of the 1972 Act where transport is divided into these artificial county slots, many of which are just not natural transport units. There is one county, for example, where 60% of the public transport journeys start on the boundary of and outside the county. When financing that transport, there is the complexity of each county imagining that it has a handling of those finances when such a small part actually comes from the funds it directly controls.

Going back to the basic principles, in the shire counties only a small part of the total money going into a bus company at the moment comes from central government and an even minuter part comes from local government. Because of that, it is necessary to start thinking on a national scale of what the passengers really want, bearing in mind that in many counties, people do not act as ratepayers when they move about. To tie the public transport system to ratepayers would appear to be unwise and in no other industry is it done.

The 1972 Local Government Act must be made to work, but it must not be pretended that anything other than the operation of transport is a local matter. Clearly the operation is, and local people, passengers and particularly the less articulate people who actually use buses, must be involved very much more, together with their elected representatives in the operation of transport. In the provision of transport some form of overview is needed. Putting under the microscope little elements of rural transport does the transport industry a disservice.

K.R. HOUNSOME (North Yorkshire County Council)

The question of the origin of the cash goes right to the roots of local government financing. It has been suggested that 70% of the cash for bus subsidies comes from Transport Supplementary Grants.

However, the Transport Supplementary Grant is only calculated on expenditure above a threshold line. Furthermore, the money paid in the Transport Supplementary Grant is knocked off the Rate Support Grant and in the coming year this is to be calculated at 61% of local government expenditure. The NBC has either to be self-supporting and get its entire revenue from the passengers, or it has to have some form of subsidy from national or local government. The Act, for better or for worse, provides that it is from local government. Mr. Smith's point on the NBC's debt is obviously one we all have some sympathy with. The Association of County Councils have been pressing the DOE and now the Department of Transport for the same treatment for the NBC as London Transport enjoyed a few years ago in the elimination of its debt. However, although it might seem easy to write off the debt to stop money going round in a circle, it does conflict with trying to show the true cost of operations. If it is done for the NBC debt, why not do it for the local authority debt? Why not do it, for example, for the housing debt, and this would reduce the problem of housing subsidies. It's all very neat and easy, but is it really correct?

A.T. BLOWERS (Bedfordshire County Council)

The financial discussion is very interesting, but it is necessary to look at other objectives. Such concepts as the community bus are worrying. It seems all very well for Norfolk to have its community bus but how many community buses are there in this country? Perhaps three?—some of which may be short-lived. A reliance on such concepts is deferring from the central issues which were highlighted in an ideological document by Oxfordshire two years ago. To quote an example 'Those who use the bus to travel to work may have to share cars, purchase their own vehicles, or at the worst change jobs'. This can be regarded

96

as rather insensitive rural planning. As Mr. Barrow stated, the issue is a political one. Oxfordshire have gone in a particular direction which may change in the future. In Bedfordshire the political opposition is not at all against its rural transport policies. In fact there is tremendous support for the rural transport policies Bedfordshire are trying to implement which are relatively cheap and, in financial terms, insignificant compared with the losses made on public transport in the urban area of Luton.

On the financial problems there really is not, as yet, much experience of manipulating the available resources and Bedfordshire have not yet straight-jacketed themselves unduly in this regard.

Finally, there is the NBC question. Two or three years ago, I wrote a series of papers suggesting the advantages of the takeover of the NBC by the counties. Although I have not totally abandoned that view, it has been modified. The bus unions pointed out that there are some counties who might simply depress the national bus industry much further. It is a sad fact that possibly the NBC is one of the defences available against a further reduction of rural bus services.

R.C. BAKER (Hawker Siddeley Dynamics Ltd.)

When public transport has been mentioned so far, it is the NBC and stage carriage services which have been implied. However, other operators and services exist: the secondary sector. They provide an extra 40% of passenger miles each year in Hertfordshire, for example. The secondary sector caters for individuals and groups but not usually for stage carriage passengers. Whilst stage carriage business is declining, the secondary sector is growing. Perhaps the secondary sector is better suited to rural areas. It is certainly necessary to include it in a discussion of this nature.

Secondly, both sectors are labour intensive but the secondary sector uses its labour much more effectively. The need for subsidy in stage carriage is related to labour productivity, so whatever standards are set for deploying subsidies these standards will need to accommodate the fact that labour costs escalate more than average costs do, so that the need for subsidy will continue to escalate.

R.C. EDWARDS (Norfolk County Council)

There are two matters dealt with too generally, the first being subsidy itself. When considering the *raison d'etre* of subsidy it is necessary to go back to when bus services generally were viable. At that time, the more profitable urban services and the better rural ones, earned sufficient money for the weaker unprofitable services to be continued and continued with overall equality of fares throughout the system. The second point is attributing the main cause of the decline of bus services to the motor car; the cause is inflation, not the car. In the context of rural mobility, most journeys now performed by motor cars were never performed by buses and were probably not performed at all. It has already been suggested that the object of a subsidy should be to subsidize the individual (i.e. the passenger) rather than the provider of transport. If so, low fares must surely be the aim, in order to keep passengers on the bus. This implies, almost certainly, an appreciably higher subsidy than at present available, but probably less outlay in the long term because passengers would be retained.

To what extent is the NBC itself helping? The county councils are being asked to increase their subsidy contributions, but nearly every year there has been some accounting manipulation which adds to the losses the counties are invited to carry by increasing subsidies. At first there was the transfer from marginal costing to operational costing, then replacement depreciation.

There has been a large increase in the express coach operations of the NBC which in 1975 showed a loss of about £4½ million. How much of that cost has been transferred from the express services to the stage? The element of cost which is allocated by the peak vehicle factor in our local NBC subsidiary is quite considerable. Two years ago 80.41% of those costs were being charged to stage carriage. Now it is 95.56%—an increase of 15%—and the amount distributed by this cost factor is just over £2 million. That means an extra £300 000 which is being transferred, rightly or wrongly, from express to stage. Probably most of the express services are desirable, but few of them are really necessary, whereas the stage carriage services on to which those costs have been transferred are in Norfolk's case, regarded as essential services.

M. MOON (Pangbourne Holdings Ltd.)

There has been a general implication that pressure groups of various kinds are undesirable and not in the public interest. However, in our kind of democracy, government is largely by pressure groups; political parties are themselves only organized by opinion. The National Bus Company should really recognize itself as a pressure group in its own right; the comments about trade union reaction to change show this up just as well. Pressure groups will continue to exist and it is important to realize this.

It is obvious that the present arrangements in rural transport are not particularly satisfactory for some parts of the rural population and we should, therefore, look at the constraints against change in this situation. There are two major constraints. One is to have Traffic Commissioners, whose remit under the various Traffic Acts is basically to act as a restrictive mechanism and to stop change by seeing abstraction where there may be none, etc. It would be better to split the Traffic Commissioner system to leave it almost as it stands for the national network (i.e. the NBC express-coach and the rail networks) and to vest their other functions in the county councils, because the county councils would deal very much more sensitively with local requirements.

A.T. BLOWERS

Secondary transport systems are largely complementary to the primary network of rural stage carriage services, which is fast disappearing in some countries. Further regard should be given to the primary route network, in the first instance, to see what flexibility is available. What extra mileage can be got out of it and what can actually be squeezed out of the system in terms of a reasonable and responsive service? This is not being done very effectively in every case.

The pattern of rural transport is extremely varied and in areas of low population is widely dispersed. To some extent what is provided in terms of public transport will dictate part of the lifestyle of the various communities. On the other hand, if the future pattern is regarded as one where certain activities are concentrated and access to facilities is obtained by using a particular standard of public transport, the situation would be more satisfactory than at present.

A concept suggested recently was the development in some rural areas of the idea of periodic markets to provide a good utilization of resources. In this case, mobile facilities and other activities would be concentrated on a different key village in a group of villages for different days of the week. A mini bus service from surrounding villages would bring people into the key village on that particular day of the week. This may sound far-fetched, but it is put forward as a good way of using very scarce resources in rural areas. Transport has to adapt to the emerging pattern of need and demand.

Fares are a critical issue at the moment. They have been rising extremely fast—much faster than the perceived cost of motoring. This is another reason why public transport is in decline. People who would normally use public transport simply cannot afford to do so and they are actually not making certain journeys they would otherwise undertake. If things continue this way, a situation may be reached where buses could break even provided millionaires travel on them and pay the fares which makes them viable. Such a situation must be avoided. There is a danger of losing passengers in the short term, but a longer term perspective needs to be created.

The role of pressure groups is difficult to define in political terms. Planners often mischievously use pressure groups to endorse the action they intend to take anyway. It is a legitimizing process and this is particularly the case with Structure Plans. The low-growth ethos that the planners have already decided upon is probably subsequently reinforced by what they find on public participation. We must recognize that pressure groups are not accountable in the way elected representatives are. They exist for specific purposes and happen to be usually very articulate. Many pressure groups put a much higher premium on amenity and environmental consideration than on other things. What is often important to people who are not in pressure groups, because they do not have time or because they do not have the knowledge or information, are more basic and fundamental things such as transport.

In theory the Traffic Commissioners ought to go now that the county councils are coordinating transport. The county councils should be able to apply standards and deal with fares policy, etc. The Traffic Commissioners can be seen as obstacles. However, in counties which are not prepared to deal seriously with the existing public transport network, it may well be true that the Traffic Commissioners are a last line of defence. Municipal bus services have been very good, their fare levels are lower, the intensity of their service has generally been higher than in comparable places. This is probably because the local councillors know they are responsible and respond to the electorate. At present, in other areas, many councillors have the excuse that any shortcomings are the NBC's fault as the counties have no direct control over the situation. For that reason there is a very clear case for more local control.

K.R. HOUNSOME

Mr. Blowers suggested that counties are not doing what he wants them to do. He must decide whether he believes in local government or not. If he does, then he has to accept that some counties will make mistakes, some will be backward and some will be leaders. The approach cannot be uniform.

Fares are certainly, high, very high in the countryside, and it is quite staggering to think of the cost of many essential journeys which country dwellers have to make. However, in an inflationary time, it is dangerous to try to hold down fares because of the multiplying effect inflation has on a deficit. It is worth reflecting on the experience of the Greater London Council whose policy of holding fares down cost about £200 million.

The reaction of the elected members serving on an Association of County Councils Committee, which considered licensing, was that the licensing powers of the Traffic Commissioners ought to come to counties, but there was a much greater reluctance to take on the running of bus undertakings. There was perhaps a feeling that it is still a job for professional management to run buses and this is perhaps best left to those that understand it. Nevertheless, the question has to be posed, what will the situation facing the bus undertakings in the UK be in, say, ten years' time? The present situation is not likely to continue. In the meantime, the 1972 Local Government Act must be made to work, unsatisfactory though it may be considered to be.

There is still much to be learned both by the bus undertakings and also by the county councils. For example, it is very unfair if a county council does not settle its bus subsidies until the financial year has already been running for a few months and then perhaps changes its policy at very short notice. People trying to run this service in difficult circumstances do deserve longer-term planning and perhaps the willingness of the local authority to share its thinking more frankly with the bus operators. On the bus undertakings side, there is a need for greater frankness on the part of some of the local managers.

G.D. NEELY

The NBC only runs 30% of the bus services in this country. It has 20 000 vehicles out of the 75 000 public service vehicles on the roads. Bus operators all work together in a confederation reasonably amicably and this in a sense, answers the suggestion that the NBC should be broken up. It is unwise to pretend that counties or districts or urban areas are little enclaves of their own. For example 27% of the bus services in Surrey are run by London Transport, in Lancashire one district council can be found inter-running with another and Greater Manchester Transport inter-running with the others, so the idea that bus services can be tied to a geographical unit is not realistic. Some municipal services do have lower fares but this is due to the money they get directly or indirectly to keep fares down.

R.C. WINFIELD (Dyfed County Council)

In practice small is beautiful. Dyfed County Council pays subsidies to more than 20 private bus operators and has sight of their accounts. These are professional bus operators who provide a service which in many cases is more effective than the National Bus Company. They definitely have a superior position in the hearts of the passengers and it is probably a reasonable claim that the morale of the staff is better than in the NBC. It is all a question of size. Almost invariably the operating costs of a proper stage carriage service with peak and off-peak services for the private operator is about 50% of what it is for NBC. The National Bus Company should talk very seriously with the trade unions about the future and should realize that in many areas they are effectively in competition with other companies who, rightly or wrongly, are thought to be providing a better service.

G.D. NEELY

It is wrong to get the impression that individual sectors of the bus industry are always in conflict with each other. The degree of harmony which exists is remarkable. The private operator, properly supervised by Traffic Commissioners for maintenance and road safety, has a very real part to play. This is particularly true in a county that has continuity of policy, but in a county with frequent changes of political control, the private operator might have a very rough time indeed if there were no ombudsman like a Traffic Commissioner to defend him. Private operators are not always successful. Recently, a private operator took over with a great flurry some of our services with ambitious promises. Six months later he was bankrupt and the councy council had to ask the NBC to run the services again.

D.R. VERNON (Greater Manchester Passenger Transport Executive)

The hypothesis that high fares drive passengers away from rural transport should be discussed. In 1972 the Greater Manchester PTE took over some of the rural services of the former North Western Road Car Co. At that time, the North Western fares followed closely the National Bus scale and were a good deal higher than fares charged by the Greater Manchester PTE. On acquisition, fares changed on the routes formerly operated by North Western and were reduced significantly by 5,6,7,8 and in some cases 9p to the Manchester fare scales. Having done so, the number of passengers remained the same. There have been similar experiences elsewhere in experiments to reduce fares and gain passengers. It can be concluded that any assumption that high fares drive passengers away, needs to be very seriously questioned.

Apart from low loadings, one of the problems of the rural services which are operated by the big operator is the dead mileage factor and it is debatable whether large organization style operation is suitable for the rural undertakings we are discussing. One man, who was the landlord of the village pub, ran a petrol station, and farmed, also kept two 29-seat Bedford coaches. These he ran a school service with and also contracted out at weekends. Should a little more encouragement be given to such people and less dependence attached to services provided by subsidized high cost organizations?

M. JACKSON (Centre for Transport Studies, Cranfield Institute of Technology)

There are two scarce resources in life: money and time. There are only 24 hours in a day for everyone and if an hour's journey faces a rural dweller going to the cinema, a two-hour round trip is added to the two-hour film. That travel time is dead time and will put quite rigid constraints on the way that person spends the rest of his 24 hours. At Cranfield, a search into mobile services was attempted to see exactly the kind of services working at the moment, the kind of people using them and how often. There is little in the literature actually dealing with mobile services and some research would be beneficial to establish their likely importance. Periodic markets seem appealing because instead of having one permanent key village in an area, there could be say four 'occasional' key villages avoiding the permanent allocation of scarce resources to one village at the expense of the rest.

A.T. BLOWERS

Firstly, on the question of fares related to inflation, it would be wrong to suggest that fares should never rise. What matters to the passenger is what he actually has to spend, not what the operational costs may be. If fares are going up faster than the cost of motoring, that does add to the problem of transferring people from one mode to the other. The other issue on fares is whether they are fixed at too high a level relative to other services. Counties should contemplate a policy of fixing fares and then relating any increases to the cost of living index. This action would, of course, have serious implications for revenue support.

The second point is the matter of standards. Public transport should be regarded as a social welfare service in rural areas and it is incumbent upon central government to make some attempt to define what that service ought to be. That would still leave open to local authorities enormous possibilities in terms of the kind of measures that could be applied in order to provide those services. Certainly, there should be no suggestion that the minimum service is the one they necessarily have to adopt.

The third point is the question of the organizational structure of the bus industry—whether the National Bus Company should be split into smaller units, whether independents should be given a free run, etc. There are probably not many independent operators who want to take over the NBC services. On the other hand, where independent operators exist, they are doing a good job. Would it be possible to obtain some coincidence between bus operators, population size and the area served by the elected-representative authority? It is likely that there is a role for the elected members to play and that they would be much more responsive and have a more positive attitude towards public transport if they were more deeply involved in actual operation than at present.

We are here to consider the future rural way of life which is intimately related to transport rather than the details of operators of conventional or unconventional services. We must not lose sight of this because if we do, we are in danger of the very kind of compartmentalization which has been criticized.

G.D. NEELY

Despite this deliberately provocative and forthright discussion, we are still in the formative stage of trying to operate within the 1972 Local Government Act which is not going to be repealed in spite of the criticism it has received. It therefore behoves everyone to try to make the eminently sensible concepts on which it was based work.

PART THREE
Public Transport Operation in Rural Areas

CHAPTER SEVEN

Priorities in Transport Policies and Programmes (TPPs)

V.A. Knight

The TPP system was introduced in 1974 in the wake of local government reorganization. Those three years have seen a significant change in the national and local economic climate, however, particularly in relation to transport expenditure. Views on the overall priority of such expenditure in national and local budgets and on individual priorities within these budgets are significantly different now from what they were three years ago, and will no doubt change by just as much again in the next three years.

In 1974 local government finance was relatively plentiful and the budget decisions and choices were partly concerned with where *expansions* of the local authority services could be provided. Although still difficult, this is not too heart-searching a process. Local government reorganization brought with it extra powers and responsibilities—and for a Shire county council not least were these relating to public transport—but coincided with, or at least closely preceded, a major downturn in national and local government finance in real terms. The problem is therefore one of increasing demands being made on a decreasing budget, and consequently one of where service cuts should be made. This is a much more onerous and politically sensitive responsibility than in determining priorities in an expanding situation.

The choice between public transport and highway development—if indeed it is a real choice at all—cannot therefore be discussed without constant reference to the financial context.

Background

The first three years of the TPP system have been accompanied by a real-terms decline in local government expenditure. Transport has suffered more than most other services, with government-accepted local authority expenditure on transport in England and Wales falling from £1202 million in 1975/76, to £1031 million in 1976/77 and to £866 million in 1977/78 (all figures at equivalent November 1976 prices). Within these totals the amounts accepted for shire counties in England were £548 million in 1975/76 and £481 million in 1976/77; the figure for 1977/78 is £378 million.

The decline in transport expenditure by Cheshire is even more severe than that experienced nationally. Their transport expenditure *per capita* was almost twice the national average at the inception of the TPP system. Thus government-accepted expenditure for Cheshire has fallen from £24.0 million in 1975/76, to £18.7 million in 1976/77 and to £13.7 million in 1977/78 (again all figures at equivalent November 1976 prices).

The Government's 1976 White Paper on Public Expenditure to 1979-80 (Cmnd 6393) proposes further reductions in local authority transport expenditure of about 10% in 1978/79. Thus there is no immediate improvement in sight.

Whilst all this 'cutting our coat according to our cloth' has been going on, the body inside the expenditure coat has been getting steadily larger. Traffic growth on highways has continued at a rate of about 5% (vehicle-mileage) per annum—with the exception of the sharp cut-back accompanying the 1974 oil crisis.

The financial situation with public transport is far from healthy. Although a number of matters affecting rail transport will be referred to later, the responsibilities of a shire county in this area are relatively limited and for most of this chapter the role of the stage-carriage bus network within the transport system will be answered. The gradual decline in bus patronage has continued, and, with increasing costs of labour, fuel and vehicles, has resulted in the cost per passenger mile escalating much faster than the general cost of living. Raising fares to cover these increased costs have caught operators in an economic dilemma, with the choice between, on the one hand, raising fares—causing passenger resistance, fall of patronage, and therefore loss of revenue—and on the other hand keeping fares down—with a guaranteed increasing deficit.

This position has been true for the rural bus services for several years preceding local government reorganization, but in recent years the previously profitable urban routes have been increasingly unable to supply an operational cross-subsidization. Thus the overall picture is of ever-increasing funds having to be poured into the bus industry to support a steadily decreasing service.

This burden of providing financial support for unremunerative bus services has, since local government reorganization, fallen very largely on the county councils. Section 203 of the 1972 Local Government Act imposed new duties on county councils, giving them responsibility to develop policies in consultation with the operators, to promote the provision of a coordinated and efficient system of public passenger transport to meet the needs of the county. The Act also enabled them to make grants towards the costs of public transport operation.

The TPP System in Principle

Against this rather gloomy financial background a new system by which the national government helps finance local authority transport expenditure has been introduced.

Prior to 1 April 1975, a large proportion of government financial help towards the cost of local transport expenditure was given in the form of specific grants. The major ones were the 75% grant towards the cost of constructing or improving principal roads and the public transport infrastructure grants received mainly by the transport undertakings. Other specific grants included those for unremunerative rural bus services and rail services, new bus purchases, and for transportation studies.

On 1 April 1975 the new 'block' grant system was introduced. Two of the main features are that the grant is based not on the actual cost of individual schemes but on county programmes of estimated expenditure backed by a comprehensive statement of transport policies; and that financial support for public transport is, in the main, channelled through local authorities and not paid directly by central government to the operators.

These county expenditure programmes, backed by a comprehensive statement of transport policies, are contained in each county council's annual submission of its Transport Policies and Programme (TPP) to the government. It is on the basis of these annual TPP submissions that the Department of Transport (previously the Department of the Environment) determines the amount of block grant—the Transport Supplementary Grant (TSG)—it will distribute to each county for the subsequent financial year.

The TPP system is therefore designed to promote the development of comprehensive transport plans by the county councils, to eliminate bias towards capital or current expenditure or towards particular forms of expenditure, and to distribute central government grant in a way that reflects as far as possible the needs of individual areas.

In order for the TPP to satisfy these basic objectives it requires an appraisal to be made of all the various aspects of transport provision, including public transport. The implications of counties' responsibilities under Section 203 of the 1972 Local Government Act 1972 have to be considered within the wider context of overall transport planning. In theory, therefore, the pre-TPP system of considering highway improvements, public transport infrastructure provision, public transport revenue support and car parking in relative isolation has been abandoned. The next section will show how well the TPP system has achieved these objectives in practice.

Although these wide ranging transport planning and coordination objectives are an essential feature of the TPP system, it must not be forgotten that the immediately over-riding purpose of each TPP submission is to enable the central government to determine the annual allocation of TSG.

The TPP System in Practice

The first fundamental change in the TPP system came soon after the first submissions (those for 1975/76). In these submissions, counties in England and Wales bid in total for one and a half times the amount of transport expenditure that was subsequently accepted for 1975/76 by the Department of the Environment. This experience led the DOE to issue expenditure guidelines for each county in conjunction with the circulars which preceded the 1976/77 and 1977/78 TPP submissions. The guidelines reflected the government's overall financial strategy as set out in the white papers (Cmnd 5879 and 6393 respectively), and were to be used by the county councils in framing their TPP submissions. The DOE asked each county to prepare a five-year 'base' expenditure programme at or below its lower guideline and if desired a 'preferred' programme at or below its upper expenditure guideline.

To a certain extent the issuing of these expenditure guidelines has removed the flexibility which counties would otherwise have had in proposing a bigger than normal five-year programme on the basis of 'need'. On the other hand the DOE has always made it clear that in theory, at least, counties could always argue the case for different levels of expenditure. On the whole, however, the issuing of guidelines has proved to be a valuable addition to the TPP system in that not only have submissions been forced to be more realistic (in the sense that the total of proposed expenditures by counties is roughly in accordance with national economic policy) but also the *accepted* expenditure programmes have in general been comparable with those submitted, thereby saving a significant amount of abortive programming work founded on unjustified optimism.

The introduction of expenditure guidelines is founded in the concept that only a finite amount of the national financial resources is available for spending on local transport. As the circular (7.1) introducing the guidelines put it, 'the Department has to distribute a fixed sum towards the needs of local authorities set out in their TPPs. More for one county means less for another. Each county's bid must be realistic if the spirit of the TSG system is to be borne out in practice'.

The second, and for rural transport the more important, change coincided with and was related to the introduction of expenditure guidelines. This change was that public transport revenue support was now to be regarded as a somewhat special part of the submission. The expenditure guidelines just referred to specifically excluded provision for financial revenue support for public transport and expenditure on new town roads. In practice this has meant that whereas the rest of a county's transport expenditure (including highway construction and maintenance, public transport infrastructure, car parking etc) has been constrained by the guidelines, proposed expenditure on public transport revenue support has been determined only by each authority's policy and its capability of financing the expenditure (assuming that the whole of it received TSG). How this affects the deciding of priorities in the TPP is discussed later. Suffice for now to say that in practice, in the 1977/78 submissions, this led the metropolitan counties to submit proposals for such large amounts of public transport revenue support outside the guidelines that, had these proposals been accepted, these authorities would have received an inordinately large share of national transport finance, to the detriment of the more rural parts of the country.

An initial complication of the TPP system, and one that affects the deciding of priorities, is that it treats capital and current expenditure together in terms of total cash flow. This treatment is in contrast to the way in which a local authority goes about its budgeting, where capital and current expenditure are handled in distinctly separate manners.

In local government, as in the private sector, the amount of capital expenditure which an authority can afford to finance is determined largely by its own estimate of its likely future ability to pay the ensuring debt charges. But because this capital financing impinges on its revenue budget only in the form of these debt charges, a local authority faced with a choice between spending a certain amount of money on a capital scheme and the same amount on a revenue item (road maintenance or public transport revenue support, for example) is bound to reflect on how differently each expenditure affects its budget. Looked at another way, when significant and immediate cuts in local government spending are required, these must come overwhelmingly from current expenditure because most of the revenue expenditure resulting from capital schemes is committed to repaying previously incurred loans.

In practice, of course, the opportunities for capital spending on public transport in rural areas are relatively few. In a shire county the majority of public transport capital expenditure is on such things as bus stations, bus/rail interchanges, bus lay-bys and turnrounds and on bus priority measures (contra-flow bus lanes for example), and of these the vast majority are located in urban areas. In Cheshire the amount spent on rural bus turnrounds and lay-bys is very small compared with the overall transport capital budget and each scheme is usually very minor in nature (i.e. less than £25 000); therefore, by and large, any such scheme which can be justified on operational or safety grounds can be constructed without great issues of priority arising.

The actual method of choosing priorities for more major capital spending varies from county to county. Some use a fairly rigorous cost-benefit approach whereas others rely on a more subjective assessment; it should not be forgotten though, that however sophisticated the assessment the final decision is the prerogative of the elected members, and therefore in essence a political one. In Cheshire, a system has been used, and is being developed, of priority assessment which judges capital transport schemes (costing over £25 000) in terms of how well they meet the agreed transportation and planning policies of the County Council. That some of the criteria used in this judgement are undoubtedly objective and measurable (e.g. accident rates, heavy lorry traffic volumes, pedestrian/vehicle conflict) should not disguise the fact that overall, subjective judgement is the critical factor.

Although there are relatively few opportunities for major capital spending on rural or inter-urban public transport, an instance has in fact recently occurred in Cheshire. The proposal was to extend into the county the electrification of two suburban rail lines radiating from Liverpool. The Merseyside PTE had intended to electrify the lines up to the county boundary, and economic assessments had shown that electrification extensions to the next major town on each line (Warrington in one instance and Chester in the other) could be justified on cost-benefit grounds. Interestingly, though, when the electrification schemes were proposed in the TPP submission, the Department of the Environment were anxious to dissuade this course of action. They indicated that if the county council were to make a capital investment in improving a rail service it would also be expected to meet the full annual revenue deficit for the service previously met by the DOE through its block grant direct to British Rail. (See Note at the end of this Chapter)

Since the county council was certainly going to have to face an increasingly large deficit for the bus system, over the next few years, it is not surprising that it was not able to commit itself in addition to a large subsidy for rail operation. The DOE's attitude was not at all conducive to enabling the county council to fulfil its public transport coordination and promotion responsibilities under the Local Government Act, nor to allowing a realistic assessment of priority between these major public transport schemes and highway proposals competing for the same capital finance allocation.

Capital spending on rural public transport has been discussed before current expenditure not because it is more important or significant, which it isn't, but rather because it is simpler to understand in the TPP context. As far as current expenditure is concerned, the bulk of it in shire counties is spent on revenue support for buses. Only in exceptional cases are non-metropolitan counties likely to contribute to the deficit financing of unremunerative rail services, and thus the rest of this discussion on public transport revenue support can be taken as applying specifically to buses.

Unlike the majority of metropolitan counties, the very many shire counties which have made increasingly significant financial contributions to public transport revenue support have not done so predominantly to keep fares down. The issue in most rural areas has been whether the services should or could be kept going at all. There have been a variety of different approaches to determining how bus services should be provided in rural areas, but the bulk of counties have started from the point of view of looking at what they already have in terms of a public transport network.

This is not to say that those counties which have based their hopes primarily on allowing private operators a relatively free rein or on the use of unconventional bus services are wrong. Indeed, flexibility in the approach to the problem is important, and undoubtedly different areas of the country will find different types or combinations of solutions more appropriate in meeting their particular problems. Nevertheless, Cheshire's approach to the issue is reasonably typical of the majority of shire counties.

Cheshire County Council's overall public transport objective is to secure the provision of a properly coordinated and efficient system of public transport to meet the basic needs of the community at minimum economic cost. The shorter term aim is to maintain that minimum level of public transport network which, particularly in less populated areas of the county, will preclude significant social hardship and can be supported from available resources.

As is typical of bus services across the country, rapidly rising costs and declining passenger numbers has meant that the county's main bus operators are facing widening deficits between operating costs and fare revenue. The county council is therefore faced with demands for increased revenue support or sanctioning considerable service reductions on the one hand, and public demands for improved services on the other. The deficit on stage-carriage bus services within the County in 1977/78 is expected to be about £1.8 million compared to an estimated deficit of £1.4 million in 1976/77 (both figures at out-turn prices). These figures would be even higher if it were not for the very significant operational cost savings already achieved or planned by operators in conjunction with the county council and the various district councils.

In pursuance of the overall public transport objective, the County's policy is to maintain a minimum level of service, particularly to the rural communities, to assist the mobility of persons not having the use of private transport. This level of service will be supported by the county council consistent with the availability of national and local financial resources. Nevertheless, in conjunction with the operators, the county is pressing ahead with attempts to rationalize services with the object of making better use of resources. The cooperation of the operators and the district councils over the past few years in reducing operating costs by selective service reductions and rationalization has made an important contribution to the fulfilment of the overall public transport policy.

In a continuing effort to reduce the public transport operating deficit by lowering the cost of operations, ways of making better use of the basic public transport resources of vehicles and crews are currently being investigated. The methods under investigation include the cutting down of peak-vehicle requirements, the rationalization of services between operators and between stage-carriage services and education transport, and the possibility of changing vehicle types. Overall transportation policies which can help reduce or at least contain the public transport deficit are being developed as part of the County Structure Plan and in local transport planning. The more important of these are the possibility of car restraint in town centres (by traffic management and car parking policies), the possibility of spreading the peak (particularly by the wider introduction of flexible working hours in offices and the staggering of school hours), and the use of bus-priority measures to alleviate existing problems of bus penetration during periods of traffic congestion.

In the county council's 1977/78 TPP (i.e. the 1976 submission), the whole of the anticipated public transport operating deficit was proposed to be met from revenue support, and was therefore included in the overall request for TSG. As explained previously, however, revenue support was excluded from the DOE expenditure guidelines, and thus the proposed expenditure under this head was in effect competing with other counties' bids for revenue support from within the national allocation and not with other items in Cheshire's TPP programme. The county council decided its bid for revenue support, therefore, on the basis of:–

(i) the savings that could realistically be made without causing undue hardship,
(ii) the fare levels, costs and patronage levels predicted by a relatively simple economic model,
(iii) the resultant calculation of the overall deficit,
(iv) a prediction as to whether this amount of revenue support could be afforded by the county council.

The implications of this are that counties did not necessarily allocate priorities to expenditure on public transport revenue support in competition with that on highways maintenance, for example, because there was no need. Thus in a rather basic way one of the main objectives of the TPP system—that of eliminating bias towards particular forms of expenditure—has been negated by a national decision.

This national decision was not necessarily wrong, but without it the shire counties, at least, would not have proposed such large amounts of revenue support in the last round of TPP submissions. What it has meant, though, is that rather than the basic decisions of priority between public transport and highway expenditure being made at the time of preparing the TPP submissions, they are being made at the time of writing as the county councils finalize their 1977/78 revenue budgets.

This chapter is therefore being written against the background of significant cuts in councils' revenue expenditure (in real terms) as a consequence of a continuing high level of inflation and of the announcement of the 1977 Rate Support Grant settlement. In Cheshire's transport budget the cuts will have to fall on one of the four main revenue heads:

   (i) staff,
  (ii) highway maintenance,
 (iii) public transport revenue support,
 (iv) revenue implications of new capital projects.

Thus it is at this stage, and not in the TPP preparation, that the real decisions of priority are being made. It would be naive, too, to think that these decisions can be made on the basis only of well founded technical argument. The truth is that when the cuts are going to hurt someone, be it staff, road users or public transport passengers, the issue is one largely of political judgement.

Cheshire Network Study

In the longer term, at least, it is inconceivable that the shire counties can afford to keep on financing public transport deficits whilst they escalate at anything like the present rate. As mentioned previously, some counties are hoping that the increasing use of unconventional services will stem the tide. In Cheshire a special public transport project team has been set up to take a fundamental look at the present bus network to see whether it is possible for changes to be made to it so that the deficit can be brought within the county council's predicted resources whilst at the same time a basic level of service is provided for towns and villages. It could be that eventually a staged but thorough and complete rationalization of present services will be needed. It is idle to presume, however, that this could be achieved without a pretty drastic upheaval for the operators and without a very careful appraisal of the effect on their labour force.

The first objective of the study was to establish options for the public transport policy of the County Council by examining the estimated effects of changes in the level of revenue support; also to suggest means of reducing the amount of revenue support payable without incurring significant hardship and to ensure any changes to the public transport network are made in the full

115

knowledge of the implications and in accordance with an overall plan.

The Department of Transport Circular of advice on Transport Supplementary Grant submissions makes it clear that submissions for bus revenue support will need in future to be accompanied by a five-year forecast. This made it all the more pertinent to link the first stage of the Study with the TPP submission. The first-stage Study Report, like the TPP, also presents a range of options on which a decision can be made.

This wider-scale approach in the first stage has meant that it was possible to take into account larger-scale changes in fixed costs over time and indeed meant it was necessary to develop a complete reassessment of costs separate from the operators' existing account system. The aim is therefore to produce a first stage report which would set out what bus networks could be obtained for given levels of revenue support, what would happen over a five-year forecasted period, and what the implications of each of these options would be in terms of population, passengers affected, other county budgets such as education, and so on.

In order to arrive at a range of eight networks for given levels of revenue support, routes were selected from a list ranked according to revenue per peak vehicle. These routes were then recosted according to a formula which takes account of the reduced level of operations. In this recosting routes are grouped into depots of an optimum size based on the most logical existing depot for that particular network. Operators other than Crosville Motor Services have been dealt with slightly differently because the change in their networks of service in Cheshire does not have a significant effect on their total level of service. Network costs were then forecasted according to an economic forecasting model.

Having established the networks the implications of each were measured in terms of mileage, vehicles, passengers carried and other statistics compared with the existing network. In addition, the route map of the network was overlaid on a population map and a measurement of population affected by service changes was made. The reduced networks would mean an increased expenditure on private contract buses by the Education Department and this was measured. Also some attempt was made to assess the implication for the Structure Plan. Finally, a cost was identified for implementing any given network, together with an assessment of the practical problems involved.

Once the first stage report of the study has been considered by the Public Transport Sub-Committee and guidelines on revenue support have been laid down, it is intended to conduct detailed area studies which would explore in greater depth the steps necessary to be taken to maintain revenue support within the guidelines. These detailed studies will attempt to get the maximum public transport mobility for a given level of revenue support which means examining every available method of public transport provision. The studies would attempt:

(i) To examine in conjunction with the operators, the viability of existing bus services and to identify where the scope for saving is greatest, and what changes in operation are required to provide the most economic result.

(ii) To assess existing and future bus travel demand.

(iii) To indicate, phase by phase, options for possible elements and levels of service and to assess the financial implications of each option in terms of cost, revenue and deficit taking account of (a) the need to reduce both the total deficit and the rate-borne contribution to acceptable levels; (b) the need to minimize social hardship arising from proposed changes in services; (c) the need to make the best use of available transport resources; (d) the county council's responsibilities for Education Transport.

(iv) To make recommendations on the policy options to be adopted, having regard to transportation and socal benefits in relation to the available support funds.

Conclusions

The basic concept of the TPP system is undoubtedly correct, in that it encourages county councils to develop comprehensive transport plans and provides a financial framework within which these plans can be brought to fruition. The individual objectives underlying the system (e.g. eliminating bias towards different forms of expenditure) are also well worth striving for. In principle, the TPP system has provided an important new dimension to transport planning and implementation, and is well worth persevering with.

What is more doubtful, however, is whether so far in practice the TPP system is meeting its objectives, especially in relation to rural public transport. There are few areas where major capital expenditure can be justified in rural public transport, and my experience is that where these have occurred, outside influences (i.e. outside the TPP system) have distorted the decision-making process. In the case of current expenditure, particularly public transport revenue support, the TPP system has not so far contributed very much to the allocation of financial priorities. Much more important in this respect have been the budgeting processes of local authorities and the subjective political decisions which are fundamental to these processes. This is bound to continue as long as the TPP system is distorted by the separate treatment of public transport revenue support outside the financial guidelines within which the rest of the county councils' transport programmes are formed. Whether this distortion has in fact contributed in a large measure to saving many rural public transport services is a moot point. One suspects that had the county councils been given a completely free hand in choosing between public transport and highways, the national rural public transport network would have suffered even further deprivations than it has in fact experienced.

Note

Subsequently the Department of Transport have stated that where a County Council wishes to improve a rail line currently operated solely to British Rail requirements, the County Council would be responsible for any *additional* operating deficits resulting from the improvement.

On the other hand, if the service is operated by British Rail on behalf of a PTE or where the proposal would be dependent on the PTE extending their supported service, the *whole* of the deficit on the line within the County would have to be met by the PTE or shared between the PTE and the County Council as though the service was operated entirely within the PTE area.

Reference

7.1 DEPARTMENT OF THE ENVIRONMENT, *Transport Supplementary Grant Submissions for 1976/7,* Circular 43/75, HMSO, 1976.

CHAPTER EIGHT

Rural Transport Coordination
Donald Awdas

The key to future passenger transport for rural communities lies in a realistic approach to planning by all those involved—the government, the local authorities, the operators and the users. Limited financial and energy resources together with reasonable land-use control will no doubt cause change to the existing systems and to the method of operating them. The duties of coordination currently imposed under Section 203 of the Local Government Act 1972 will need to be exploited in order to satisfy the transport requirements of the rural dweller in line with the level of service available to his urban counterpart. All the differing parts of the transport system will require welding together into a comprehensive whole so as to satisfy the essential trips for journey to work, education, shopping, health, social and leisure purposes. A separate approach to each mode and to each activity is likely to prove to be too costly in the long run and attitudes of operators and users are going to have to change to accommodate this. It will be necessary to exploit novel and unconventional systems which are proved to be economically sound and operationally practical, and the experience of our European neighbours should be monitored in order to establish value for money transport. The Government's Transport Policy Document has opened the way, and the resulting White Paper will need to grapple with the failure of passenger transport in the rural areas. New and enlightened policies giving local authorities real power and appropriate resources to solve the problem will be necessary if the fast approaching crisis is to be averted.

This chapter reviews some current transport and land-use planning problems (8.1), relationships and responsibilities of local authorities and operators and looks more specifically into travel concessions and school transport operation in the UK. Current practice in other European countries is glanced at in order to see how systems and operations compare.

The need for a new approach to planning and providing transport in the rural areas has been recognized by all accepting that too many people are still without essential services such as transport in this modern society. It might well be considered that this approach would lead to a reversal of current planning trends, and possibly that the limited resources available to us would not permit such a policy, however ideal. The trend towards centralization of facilities does imply that the rural dweller is less well-off than his urban counterpart. In the rural areas today the lack of facilities is not likely to be improved, and even if public transport at prices that people can afford would act as a reasonable substitute, it is unlikely that such improvement will materialize in the foreseeable future. Since 'adequate rural bus services cannot be provided except as a result of some measure of financial assistance from outside the industry', and government have already declared their policy to be one of reduction in financial support to public transport generally, it might be considered that the future is far from bright. However the government has stated its intention 'to provide reasonable mobility for the large minority without cars' (8.2). Surely such intentions are of interest and directly applicable to those residing in rural areas.

TABLE 8.1   Public Passenger Transport in Devon

BRITISH RAIL

1960   401 miles Track   131 Stations / Halts open

1975   191 miles Track   43 Stations / Halts open

9.75 million passengers carried

Subsidy approx £2½ m per annum

BUSES

NBC (and predecessors)	Miles Operated	Vehicles	Passengers
1955	29 m	775	110 m
1960	26 m	731	89 m
1965	25 m	733	76 m
1970	23 m	676	59 m
1975	14 m	435	55 m
			(Estimate)

120

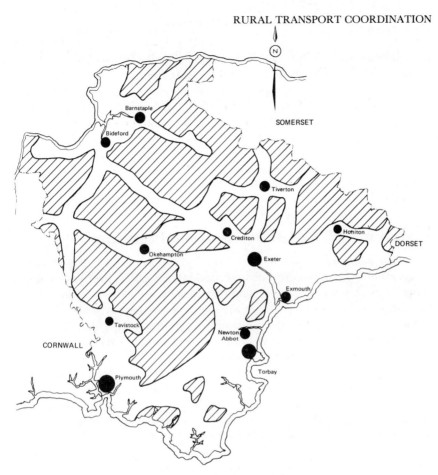

Figure 8.1   Devon County Council Transport Policies and Programmes.
Areas with less than a daily bus service shown shaded.

The existing transport system reflects the economic and social development of the past, and often this does not match up with the demand placed upon it today. The inadequacies of the past and existing systems are all too apparent, and probably do not provide the right background on which to base plans for the future mobility of rural dwellers. Transport usage and provision has changed dramatically over the last two decades with a significant decline in public transport—both road and rail (Table 8.1). This has also been reflected throughout Europe and the Western World. The changes in the social and economic climate have become very pronounced and people's demand for transport has undergone a marked shift in favour of private travel. Public transport is now often seen only as the 'insurance' against failure of the private means of travel. For the majority of the population, however, it still provides an

121

essential means of mobility. Mothers with small children, the elderly, handicapped, and those going to and from school and other places of education, still need to rely on public transport, because they have no access to private transport. There are also those who are precluded from driving on grounds of not holding a valid driving licence who also require public transport. It is perhaps accessibility to other essential services rather than mobility which needs additional stress. To be able to get to work, to school, to the doctor's surgery and to the shops are more important than to be able to travel anywhere as far as the rural dweller is concerned. Leisure, although important, is only of secondary significance.

Problems of Rural Settlement Planning

Passenger transport is a human need and it is generally agreed that one answer to the problem of provision of adequate back-up services for the rural community is by establishing a policy of centralization of a 'key settlement' nature. To be effective and successful it is necessary to coordinate the provision of all major services, particularly health, education, highways and public transport amongst others. Transport is one of the essential services and its role is vital to the success of the centralization policy as a whole. As well as the bus, it should be recognized that rail branch lines and ferries can act as a necessary link in the transport chain, thereby giving access to the people living in such areas. In the past withdrawal of transport facilities, particularly rail closures, have caused considerable inconvenience. Problems of providing rail replacement bus services are well known, and the inadequacy of such services has been studied and commented on by the South West Transport Users Consultative Committee (8.3). Since 'closure of a branch line is the largest single change in land use which may be made without planning consent' it is perhaps not surprising that so many problems have been experienced as a result. There does seem to be a case for making British Rail answerable to the local community, as well as to central government, as are other providers of public transport, for it can hardly be said that the TUCC has any teeth when it comes to handling such matters, despite their right to call for an inquiry into proposed closures. It must also be understood that 'virtually all train services have become highly uneconomical'.

As with all public transport services, those developed jointly by the local authority transport planners with the operators, should provide more suitable answers to future problems. In the past, such joint interest was not always apparent, and the user suffered as a result. The planners cannot ignore public transport issues in the future, since local plans and structure plans will need to reflect the concern for public transport in the countryside. To achieve acceptance, there will also be a need to demonstrate that the public have been directly consulted over the problems, and that the solutions reflect a measure of public participation, prior to being accepted and implemented. Thus the user can have a big say in the services that directly affect him, should he choose to do so. The Development Plans of the past have often largely ignored public transport issues; the future should prove to be different. Public transport in one form or another helps to overcome hardship, and is necessary to assist in the economics of a village community. Such provision may not, of course, follow previously accepted practice; and provision may not be in a traditional form, but that which is provided will have to meet local needs as cheaply as possible.

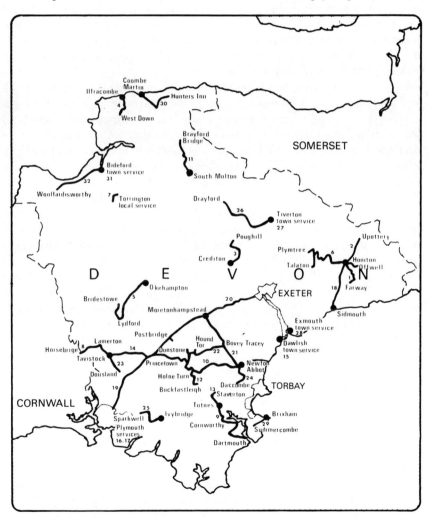

Figure 8.2   Devon—32 experimental bus services, 1976

123

The education needs of a community are not satisfied purely by carrying children to school, for quite often adults' requirements are equally as great, particularly after retirement age has been reached. Transport for those wishing to join in further education pursuits is not always easy to provide, but such needs must be considered in planning communities, particularly 'key villages'. Such requirements should be given adequate consideration when transport is being rationalized, or withdrawn, from a rural area. The idea that rural dwellers should survive on lifts from helpful neighbours for their essential needs, is ignoring the real possibility of hardship for such residents. This is not to forget the part that properly authorized car schemes can play in serving a local community, but such schemes require to be paid for in a proper manner. It should not mean that a local authority is abdicating its responsibilities by seeking public transport on the cheap.

Due to the increasing cost of petrol, the problems caused by urban overspill and development are diminishing as far as the rural community is concerned. Commuters are no longer prepared to travel so far to their work-place, and public transport seldom serves their needs should they wish to travel far away from the local settlement, on a regular daily basis. It is necessary to develop and expand local industry, in order to keep the countryside as an effective economic unit, and often tourism or recreation can be exploited to serve the rural area, thus compensating for the withdrawal of agriculture or other local industry. Such action will help to prevent the area becoming sterile, and will mean that large areas of the rural countryside do not become places of total isolation for the residents. Quite often sensible planning of leisure and recreational transport can help to compensate, at least on a seasonal basis. This will help to reduce the total cost of provision for public transport services in the area, throughout the year. As with these services the provision of other jointly utilized vehicles, such as postal minibus and other freight/passenger combinations, must be considered so that improved vehicle utilization and minimum cost can be achieved. Although motorways and similar road developments have been considered to be wholly detrimental to the rural dweller, in some cases they can be beneficial. Trunk services may be speeded up thus allowing them more time to divert through villages, thereby giving them a much needed transport facility at minimum cost to the operator and to the local authority.

Relationship and Responsibilities

The existing structure of the transport industry is unlikely to remain unless costs are radically trimmed, and approaches to service planning are changed. A fragmented industry with its nature of high operating costs, cannot be sustained in the longer term: however an organization coordinated at too high a level is unlikely to fare much better. A regional type structure should bring greater economies and provide a better service to the user at the same time. This should allow companies to be large enough to reap some economies of scale, but not too large to cause undue management problems such as poor industrial relations and a general lack of communication, which is apparent in large organizations. Effective marketing and promotion of all types of passenger, and possibly linked-freight movement, is a prerequisite for a sound public transport business, which adequately serves the passenger.

Partnership between the operators and the local authorities, as already established under the TPP procedures, must develop and joint planning and decision-making holds out some hope for future success. The 1977 White Paper (8.4) has much to say on this. Plans must endeavour to arrest the present fall in ridership and encourage passengers to remain with an effective transport system. An improved service, which is totally reliable, is one way of arriving at such a situation. Some restraint, possibly through traffic measures and petrol pricing, should help to improve transport generally and this should lead to some benefit for the rural areas. Restraint, if imposed, will be unpopular and is not likely to prove acceptable, so public transport will have to succeed. Perhaps this will only prove to be possible if competition is eliminated in the bus industry, although the experience of the railways does leave much to be desired as a result of the elimination of competition.

Public transport in the rural areas is provided by a vast number of different operators and individuals, and until Section 203 of the Local Government Act 1972 was enacted, no one authority was deemed to be responsible for the coordination of the activities of all the various bodies involved in the provision of public passenger transport. Transport can be provided by bus operators in the public and private sectors, in which is included the municipal operators. They provide stage carriage and express services in addition to contracts, private hire, excursion and tours. British Rail provide services particularly on branch lines, which tend to serve the rural countryside. Taxis and private hire cars serve shorter distance travellers and often act as a link between the other transport modes. Other public bodies such as the Post Office, area health authorities, education authorities and social services produce yet another transport system often superimposed on that provided by those already mentioned. By adding the services operated by the WRVS and Women's Institutes and other voluntary bodies it becomes a positive nightmare to consider that any one authority can effectively coordinate transport in the rural parts of this country. Many trips are made by passengers in private cars taken in the form of lifts in addition to these other trips.

However, the need for coordination certainly exists, and the need for a controller in this jungle of transport provision has now been recognized. In the larger metropolitan areas integration is deemed to be essential, hence the establishment of passenger transport authorities. Is there not a case for seeking something akin to the more scattered rural communities? Even the Traffic Commissioners cannot adequately control the services of all these transport operators, although they do regulate some of the competition, but they cannot make provision for both demand and need, even if they could establish that such exists. Now with the new legislation the county councils have been given that awesome task of bringing all the interested parties together in order to see that the needs of the user are properly provided for by the various operators. The right mix of service cannot be provided without there being established an effective joint partnership in planning as well as in funding for the whole transport enterprise. Consultation between the providers and the users, represented by the local authority, is essential as is consultation between these two and the Traffic Commissioners who act as regulators for a large part of the transport system. These same regulators have a duty to coordinate services and this could well conflict with the new role given to county councils by Section 203. This requires counties to develop policies to promote the provision (by others) of a coordinated and efficient public transport system to meet the needs of the county. Thus in order that this can become effective there is a necessity for the counties and the Commissioners to come much closer together with the latter becoming more mindful and concerned with the policies of the former. In time this will come about, probably without the one suppressing the other.

Together with Section 203 a new financial arrangement has been evolved by

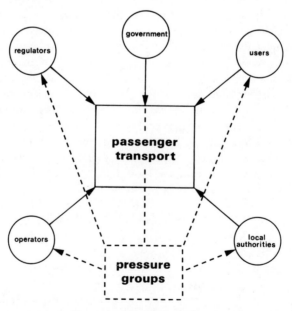

Figure 8.3 Passenger transport environment.

the government which produces the ability for the county councils to meet the needs of transport operators through grants in aid of public services. Such grants are made after approval by the Secretary of State, through the annual Transport Policies and Programmes (TPP) submission. Thus the duty to coordinate and the power to fund public transport have been added together and this arrangement causes the operator, the customer and the regulator to be drawn into a closer relationship to ensure that the user is provided with the type of service that he needs. The TPP cannot be produced effectively unless all parties are generally in agreement and thus the document itself represents their joint efforts and aspirations.

Similar relationships have evolved in the urban areas through the Land Use Transportation Studies, and now the rural areas are linked within a joint exercise also. Attitudes to public transport and its support are the topic of joint meetings and officers work closely to produce a rounded system of public transport for all users. Working on local plans and on the Structure Plan makes the team approach even more meaningful and important. Experiments are prepared and executed jointly, and operators are compelled to assist in the establishment of transport policies and plans for the future since their own existence is closely linked to the results of such exercises. Thus operators need to be ready and willing to experiment, in order to improve services where it can be demonstrated that there is some hope of a satisfactory result ensuing. All this demands that both local authorities and operators have a sufficiency of adequately trained and qualified transport planners so that plans can be executed in line with agreed and approved policies. Any lacking on either side means that the customer is the loser initially, and the operator is likely to miss out in the longer term since the network will not be viable and may not even survive. Finance is the lubricant by which the partnership is maintained and operators cannot do without the support that the local authorities can provide through a well presented TPP. Both sides have a direct interest in the provision of a basic transport network to serve the needs of the community, and both are intensely interested in suitable levels of service, since satisfaction is derived from them by the employee in public transport, and by the traveller, for without him the operator would not exist either.

Concessionary Fares

Local authorities are given the statutory right to offer travel concessions to specific groups of society by Section 138 of the Transport Act 1968. Similar groups are referred to in the Consultation Document. It should be remembered that such power to offer travel concessions is discretionary and that at the present time one sixth of the non-metropolitan districts do not choose to offer any facilities, presumably because they do not feel that they can justify such expenditure. Only four county councils offer countywide schemes at the present time. The Act allows local authorities to reimburse the whole cost or to make a contribution to any cost incurred for concessions to certain well defined groups of people, these being men over 65 years of age, women over 60 years of age, blind persons and those with disabilities or injuries which seriously impair their ability to walk. This concession is defined as 'the reduction or waiver of a fare or charge either absolutely or subject to terms, limitations or conditions' and is generally made available through a system of tokens, vouchers or passes. Despite this power to offer concessions, it is not really the answer. Most people would prefer to pay their way as a result of having sufficient money to pay for services received.

The cost of such schemes are specifically excluded from Transport Supplementary Grant payments to local authorities, yet with the subject now attaining even greater importance it may be that this situation will change once consultation on transport policy is completed. The schemes that do exist would seem to demonstrate their complexity and illustrate the wide variation that persists between schemes, and it is said by the Association of District Councils that 'schemes depend on the attitude of the National Bus Company Subsidiary in the area' (8.5). As the result of a recent Survey of all the schemes nation-wide, the Association has recommended to its members that they seek to establish 'uniform schemes within a County operated by Districts', where a district is willing to participate in such a scheme. This is perhaps not so surprising, seeing that there are so few county run schemes.

In these inflationary times the cost of such specific concessions as permitted under the Transport Act needs to be considered, since they have doubled since 1973-74 and are currently costing in excess of £75 million. The Government however, feel that they can be used effectively as an instrument of social policy since—where concessionary fares are made available to O.A.P.'s the benefits are likely to go predominantly to poorer people.

However, this high cost operating mainly to the benefit of the people residing in metropolitan areas, and therefore at the expense of rural dwellers, cannot continue to rise at the same rate. Nevertheless, it does help to alleviate the general rising costs of fares to certain vulnerable members of society, when transport subsidies are being reduced generally.

The Consultation Paper poses the question—'Should concessionary fares on buses be provided in accordance with some common framework or should local authorities continue to exercise full discretion?'

This recognizes the disparity of provision which possibly leads to unfairness when comparing schemes offered by different local authorities. The government have therefore been led to establish a Working Party to examine the current practice with a view to holding further discussions on the means of maximizing the social benefit offered by these specific travel concessions enumerated in the Transport Act 1968. The declared aim is to seek value for money with such subsidy, but will all areas benefit to the same extent by having a unified national scheme? Surely rural dwellers will lose out purely because they do not have the same facility for travel as their urban counterpart. It is possible that increased subsidy for concessionary schemes could be paid at the expense of additional subsidy to the rural network and once again people residing in rural areas could lose out.

In Scotland the need to rationalize the schemes inherited at the time of reorganization has been recognized. However, the ability to pay for any

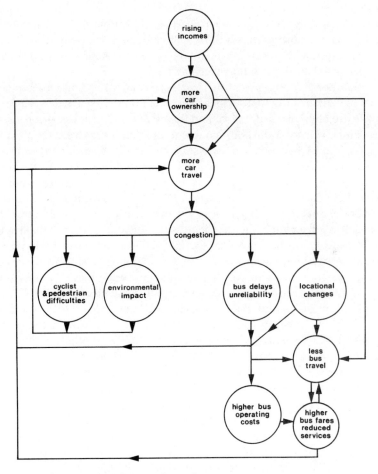

Figure 8.4   The dynamics of personal travel

   Source: 'Changing Direction'—a report for the Independent Commission on Transport, Coronet Books, 1974

129

possible changes has not as yet been authorized. This tends to demonstrate the dilemma for anyone seeking to change the existing system. The keeping of responsibility at local level whilst at the same time relying on the government to make the necessary funds available, particularly at a time of inflation, and when schemes need to be brought on to a common basis, does not make decision making any easier for the operator or for the local authority. National standards are generally acceptable, providing that adequate national resources are generated to implement these standards.

The government has stated that it intends to provide for financial stability for both the operators and for local authorities and that increases in subsidies for concessionary fares have not been ruled out. However, it has also stated that other areas of transport expenditure will have 'to accommodate an adequate level of selective support', as might be given to those in receipt of travel concessions. Does the rural dweller pay again?

On average 48% of those entitled to concessionary travel take up the offer but the actual figures fluctuate widely between areas. Nevertheless, since those eligible are often disadvantaged, and therefore from the lower income groups, they can benefit from the additional mobility that results from the concession. The National Consumer Council have called for 'a nationally constituted scheme of transport concessions' which is supported financially by the Government. It is said that this should be a unified system comprising a minimum national standard with common facilities available throughout the country and therefore available for all journeys whether as a resident or a visitor. Local authority involvement in such a scheme is envisaged since it is felt that transport should continue to be controlled locally. If this is the case why have clearly defined national standards of provision? It will not be possible to give everyone the same degree of benefit, for those residing in rural areas will suffer because the costs of travel are generally higher per mile. To achieve common standards, common fare scales and pricing policies will be needed which would entail scales set by the government so that a common tariff is available irrespective of the operator or ownership. This would have to apply to both the public and the private sector and is hardly in keeping with the notion of local control.

John Hanson (8.5) has stated that it is more important to maintain bus routes rather than to extend concessionary bus passes for the elderly. After all in a rural county such as Devon, a concessionary ticket with no network is not of very much use to the holder. There is a fear that the elderly and other disadvantaged people could become isolated since operators might not be able to afford to run some services, or even routes, should subsidy be reduced. This raises the whole question of discrimination in the payment of subsidy. Elsewhere in the country it has been suggested that if bus companies do not offer concessions then subsidies should not be paid for unremunerative services. Would more revenue from the increase in the number of those travelling with concessions offset the loss of revenue? It is very doubtful, since a 50% concession requires a 100% increase in travellers to keep the service earning the same amount of revenue.

School Transport Operations

School transport needs should be regarded as an integral part of the public transport system. An education authority has a duty to provide transport between home and school, free, under Section 55 of the Education Act 1944. Such a duty means that a significant part of the total passenger movement in rural counties is performed as school transport. This tends to run at the peak times of operation. The costs of this service have been rising over the past decade and it is likely that they will continue to rise in the immediate future. In most areas costs have doubled since reorganization. With this background, there is a need to ensure that such movement is closely coordinated with other public transport services, be they contracts, stage carriage or private hire.

In the early 1950s schools transport did not provide the major means of income for operators since most of them had a great deal of private hire work, often in addition to running garages and/or haulage or removal businesses. There was then much competition for school contracts and keen tendering persisted. Invariably the lowest tender was automatically accepted. Since such times, largely due to the increase in the use of the private car, this mainstay of business has largely diminished. With it, the size of undertakings has also reduced and many under-capitalized operators are now finding it impossible to continue in service when their vehicles need replacing. As in many other fields of commerce, inflation has caught up with them, and they cannot find funds to replace vehicles, to pay the high costs of running repairs or for the employment of full-time drivers.

The high cost of wages must be borne in mind since they generally form 50–70% of the total cost of operation. Drivers may not be effectively employed outside the times of running children to and from school, and so become an excessive burden on any operator. Part-time drivers, although suitable in theory, are not always readily available, or suitably qualified or trained. Thus this scarcity of money, satisfactory vehicles and sufficient qualified drivers, means that the planning of transport for school operations must be given high priority in order to bring about effective crew and vehicle utilization for without it, it will not be possible to reap physical and financial economies. When new schools are planned, or others disposed of, or when school hours are due to be changed, it is necessary to involve those responsible for transport, at an early stage in the deliberations, otherwise costs can escalate, and individuals can be put to much inconvenience.

The ideal arrangement when employing an operator for school contracts, is

131

to arrange for such work to take place alongside other existing work such as other contracts, private hire (although limited), stage carriage (often subsidized), in order that one part of the business can be used to cross-subsidize another. This is quite reasonable and also helps to hold down the annual increasing costs which have been rising at a rate of approximately 20% per annum over the last few years. Where possible such operators should be encouraged to take on other school work, like trips to playing fields, swimming baths and any other school activities, thereby keeping the business viable and at the same time keeping costs down for the local authority. Generally speaking this type of working will be cheaper than an education authority providing its own vehicles, and it should help to ensure that all vehicles and crews are of P.S.V. standards, which improve the safety aspect when carrying children.

In any local authority those responsible for school transport provision must work very closely with those planning public transport generally. It is preferable if the person responsible can exercise direct control over both aspects, thus producing the most cost effective transport for the county and its ratepayers. In some instances, by putting more school children on to season tickets this might allow a stage carriage service to become viable, thereby allowing the service to be retained in the network. Such action could certainly help to keep a route operating within an authority's subsidy criteria. This action would be to the benefit of all local people residing within the area. At other times the public can be allowed to use empty seats on school contract vehicles, where such are available. A permit granted by the Traffic Commissioners under Section 30 of the Transport Act 1968, allows this to happen. This type of coordination helps to keep costs down and allows for greater public provision. There are limitations on the use of such arrangements since many of the potential passengers do not like to travel at such early hours, and others find that the long delay between going to school and returning, gives too long away from home. Nevertheless, there is some help to those who reside in the depths of the countryside, away from service facilities. This helps to demonstrate how school transport operations can be dovetailed in with the total requirements for transport for passengers within the county as a whole.

Because the transport industry is labour intensive, there has been a sharp rise in unit costs recently. There are few economies of scale that can be utilized within the industry as a whole, particularly now that more people travel by private transport than by public transport. In order to maintain existing standards, costs are bound to rise during such times of inflation. Labour costs are currently rising at a rate above the increase in the cost of living, and other costs are keeping up with the generally high rate of increase at this time. Consequently, operators are seeking frequent renegotiation of rates for both contracts and season tickets. Fares applications from the major operators are tending to be bi-annual, thereby pushing up costs even higher. All services

132

require meticulous and continuous monitoring if costs are to be kept to an acceptable minimum. Despite this, a reasonable amount of renegotiation and a limited amount to tendering help to keep increases within acceptable limits. Full tender procedure in many rural counties would tend to make costs rise even faster, particularly where there is little or no competition. Such action is unlikely to be in the best interests of the authority and could be said to be acting against coordination as required by Section 203.

There may be a case for a limited amount of use of county-owned vehicles, especially in difficult areas where operators do not exist, or where considerable payments are needed to cover dead mileage on contracts. This form of operation is seldom cheap, and the economics of using such vehicles needs close scrutiny. Currently a county council is not able to act as a public transport operator since it cannot operate for hire and reward. This means that the vehicles that it uses for school operations can often be under utilized and are not available to the general public. The need to coordinate such work with the essential tasks of carrying school meals is essential, and a policy for purchasing jointly used vehicles should be followed. There is possibly a case for looking for employment with social services commitments, where suitable vehicles can be found for all these multifarious tasks. Some relaxation of the licensing laws would obviously aid local authorities in carrying out their tasks under Section 203, recognizing, of course, that they should not set up in opposition to established operators, but rather to complement their services. The clauses in the Road Traffic Bill 1974 would have helped local authorities in their task as coordinators of public transport, had the Bill been enacted.

It should be stressed that if operators, particularly the Independents, become too tied to a county council, then that authority will suffer with any rise and fall in the operator's fortunes. Somehow there needs to be a happy compromise where both the bus operator and the county benefit without either being over-committed to the other. Through joint working, an improved service should become available for schools, and the public at large should benefit not least those residing in rural areas.

In the consultative document (8.7), school travel has been reduced in importance by being mentioned in only one paragraph in the whole publication. Seeing that it is already responsible for expending greater sums of public money than the total cost of bus subsidies in the shire counties, its place would not appear to be fully recognized by those in government responsible for public transport. In practice the document issued by the Department of Education and Science (8.8) has no further purpose and it would be totally wrong to say that the general policy on statutory school transport is under review. The review has been completed and no alternative approach has been considered suitable. In practice operators are already withdrawing concessions to school children who are forced to travel at the peak. In planning terms, a complete new 'think' on the whole area of catchments and staggered hours would seem to hold out better prospects for containing costs and improving the service generally than do aspects of limiting charging to some members of the community. If school transport was to be considered as a full part of the total transport network, then provision could be totally coordinated, public transport could be utilized to the full and possibly at a cheaper total cost than it represents today.

Concessionary fares for school children need to be considered too, since the free provision of transport for some children can affect the payment of supplementary benefit to some disadvantaged parents, and these fall outside the categories of entitlement already mentioned. It has been advocated that such concessions should remain until the child leaves school, but that age can vary, dependent upon the schooling offered within different local authorities. School ceases for some at 16 years and for others not until 18 years—where would minimum national standards apply in this case?

In addition to these specific concessions, others are offered by the operators, both road and rail, which are generally based on age, school attendance, regular travel (season tickets), off-peak travel or for other specified purposes, and these are established as part of the marketing and pricing policy of the transport undertaking. In some instances these facilities, which may have been available for a considerable period, are now being withdrawn. Such is the case where they have been to the benefit of people travelling at peak hours, where the costs of operation are very much higher than at other times. Local Education Authorities are being particularly badly hit at this time by this. British Rail have just announced that their school children's concessions will not be available after the 1976/77 school year. This might well cause a county council to alter its policy for moving children from and to school, particularly if private bus operators can be used at less expense to the ratepayers. Such independent action by British Rail does, however, tend to act against the spirit of coordination for which counties have been striving since local government reorganization. It must be realized that this is just one of the ways in which operators have been forced to act in order to recoup some of the increasing costs at this time. Despite this they are generally conscious of the effect of loss of revenue from reduced levels of ridership due to a continuing process of increasing fares to cover escalating costs, causing a spiral, and both the user and operator tend to lose out in the long run (see Fig. 8.4).

Some European Experience

Despite recent decline, public transport trips per head of population in Britain remain high relative to those in other European countries. The use of public transport in such countries as Norway, Germany, Benelux and Sweden is high, and is increasing, but this is largely due to urban development in the main. In France, however, funds are only contributed to infrastructure, and other development in support of the urban developments and on inter-city schemes. Local public transport is generally poor since transport provision tends to respond to development rather than guide it, and French rural networks suffer as a result. In Germany local transport is regarded as an essential public service since it is recognized that it improves the environment and enhances the quality of life. Funds are made available to modernize the bus fleet and there has been a doubling of revenue support over the period 1970/1974. The fleet replacement support is similar to the existing New Bus Grant provision in the United Kingdom. In Europe generally there is a fairly stable level of bus patronage. Fares tend to conform to national government policy, unlike the UK and in Holland in particular fares are subsidized in order to keep them in line with the general rise in the cost of living. Unlike Europe, the situation in North America demonstrates the lack of public transport, particularly in the rural areas. In some cases the need to replace it has been realized, and the cost of doing so is prohibitive, which tends to suggest that it is better to try and retain as much of the existing network as possible, because of the inordinate cost of re-provision at a later date. This supposes that the network remaining is worth support in the first place.

The system in Switzerland, Germany, Norway and Sweden is most like that which pertains in Britain, except that joint use services, particularly with schools and the post office, are exploited to a far higher degree. In Norway the system is largely administered from the centre, and maximum fares are controlled by the Government. Subsidies are paid to support the existing network serving rural communities, but the level of these subsidies are regarded as being generally low $(12\frac{1}{2}\%)$ in comparison to costs. Revenue on the bus system is largely earned from school passenger services and freight, both of which contribute about one third of total revenue. In addition, joint freight/passenger and mail/passenger services are used to the full, which helps local communities to a high degree. This also means that costs are apportioned over more than one activity, thus producing better economics for the network as a whole.

Sweden probably comes closer to our own system than any other country. In Sweden, transport planning and town planning are well developed, and already integrated. Subsidies are made available to operators handling school contracts as well as for social services which is very much in keeping with that country's approach to social welfare planning and policies. Many rural bus services are operated by the State Railway, and this tends to improve the planning of the connections between main and feeder networks, as well as producing high quality information in the form of timetables and market information generally. Travel concessions are available nationally to the old age pensioner and to handicapped people, which allows them to travel twice a week for essential shopping trips. This is an improvement on Britain in this field. Linked services for passengers, freight and mail are provided, and a sophisticated costing system is applied nationally.

Because the railways operate much of the rural and inter-urban network in Sweden there is a greater ability and desire to replace discontinued rail branch line services, since all passengers contribute to the overheads of the one undertaking. In addition, there are many small independent operators but only two large ones. Many cars are operated instead of buses on the feeder services where demand is low. Grants are made available on losses only, and these are limited, but travel concessions aid operators significantly in their bid to break even. School travel concessions are paid, but the vehicles on which they apply are not available to the general public. As a result, variable sizes of vehicles are operated and most roads have some sort of service even where very low demand is experienced (and this is said to be as low as 3 passengers in 14 days). The Post Office also use cars extensively in remote areas, thereby keeping costs down. Dial a bus and other diversionary pick-ups are used, and coordination with fixed line routes and feeder services are planned in advance.

The feeder services are available at least once per week, and they are timed so as to allow one round trip to the nearest major centre with adequate time for shopping and a guaranteed return trip the same day. They link in with the line routes operated between major centres. When costs exceed revenue, having taken into account subsidy, then services or routes are rationalized.

In Denmark strategic planning aims at optimizing existing services by providing for a minimum level of service at minimum cost. This tends to demonstrate a value for money approach similar to that advocated in the Transport Policy Document. It is suggested that licensing and standards generally are more lax than in the United Kingdom but that this allows for flexibility in planning and operating the whole network. Perhaps the system in this country would have a longer life span if this could be accommodated here. The planners are attempting to measure the quality of service by modelling such aspects as:- journey time, frequency, the walking distance, working hours, travel time, waiting time and accessibility, but this may apply mainly to the urban rather than the rural scene. Staggered working hours are all part of the way of life and this will tend to help those planning transport for passengers. It is recognized that the disadvantaged, who are in the minority, should have public transport and that car ownership does not preclude members of households other than the driver from using public transport. In the rural areas facilities are not as good as in the urban areas but demand is recognized as being lower, and is planned for accordingly. As in UK it is said that people adapt to the withdrawal of public transport. Standards are defined locally by study groups who also help plan the provision of services based on known demand and they therefore participate and plan with these limitations in mind.

136

Conclusions

It is perhaps consoling to the transport coordinator that some sort of bus service has generally survived where the demand is anything like sufficient to justify one. Most local authorities recognize this and still provide accordingly, but it is doubtful if this can satisfy need for all time. 'Need' recognizes the social cost benefit to the disadvantaged whereas 'demand' often reflects only specific use at a particular time. It is necessary to look at both when planning services for the rural community, for the bus, like the train may prove to be highly uneconomic, and yet people must have access by some means to other essential services.

It is unlikely that grant aid at existing levels can be maintained indefinitely, and some rationalization is considered to be essential. Cost effectiveness and efficiency of future systems will be as important as social justification, since if these do not prevail, then there is unlikely to be much opportunity to satisfy social need. As in the rest of Europe, rural services cannot remain without financial assistance, recognizing that it is almost impossible to generate sufficient revenue to make them self-supporting. Changes which help to keep the high cost of labour to a minimum will prove necessary, and the use of volunteer drivers will have to be exploited to the full. The rural transport experiments will no doubt seek to maximize on these and similar opportunities. The existing law will have to be reviewed and interpreted more flexibly, or even ultimately changed, so that it can cope with today's conditions and not those of earlier days. Finding solutions that are acceptable to all parties will not be easy, but further flexibility is essential, if public passenger transport is to continue to serve those without access to the private car. Experimentation would have to become an integral part of operations in order to ensure future success, and different patterns of service not currently permitted would need to be tried and evaluated without operator bias.

All this would probably require that investment in transport would be equated to quantified demand possibly through a process of modelling similar to that used in the urban transportation studies. The coordinator of transport will have to understand the realistic cost of the services he seeks to provide or have provided by others. Generally he will require these to be as cheap as possible, consistent with a high standard of safety and at lowest environmental cost to the community as a whole.

References

8.1 See also HIBBS, J., *The Bus and Coach Industry,* Dent, 1975; THOMAS, D.St.J., *The Rural Transport Problem,* Routledge & Kegan Paul, 1963; TURNS, K., *The Independent Bus,* David & Charles, 1974: WHITE, P.R., *Planning for Public Transport,* Hutchinson, 1976

8.2 DEPARTMENT OF THE ENVIRONMENT, *Transport Policy—A Consultation Document*, 2 Vols, HMSO, 1976

8.3 TRANSPORT USERS CONSULTATIVE COMMITTEE, (South west area), *Buses as Replacement for Discontinued Rail Service*, A Report, 1976

8.4 *Transport Policy* (Cmnd 6836), HMSO, 1977

8.5 ASSOCIATION OF DISTRICT COUNCILS, *Provision of Transport in Rural Areas*, 1974 and *Concessionary Fares—A Report*, 1975

8.6 HANSON, J., 'The Importance of Country Bus Routes to the Elderly', *Western Morning News*, 12 November 1976

8.7 MINISTRY OF TRANSPORT, *Road Traffic Bill*, HMSO, 1974

8.8 DEPARTMENT OF EDUCATION AND SCIENCE, *School Transport*, (The Hodges Working Party Report), HMSO, 1973

CHAPTER NINE

Rural Rail Services

P.A. Keen

It is not easy, in the context of British Rail in 1977, to characterize a rural railway. Forty years ago it would have been straightforward. The coverage of small towns and villages en route was fairly comprehensive and it would even have included the extensive and supremely uneconomic duplication of facilities by competitive companies which extended to such unlikely places as Cromer and Wisbech, to Launceston and Blaenau Ffestiniog.

Since that time there has been a process of closure of rural branch lines which began in fact soon after nationalization but was greatly accelerated during that period which has come to be known as the Beeching era. In the years following 1963 about 3000 miles of predominantly rural route were closed to passenger traffic. At the same time a large number of intermediate stations were closed on main lines. In these latter cases the inherently uneconomic character of the local services providing for rural stations was reinforced by operating considerations. A slow train amongst fast trains occupied a disproportionate amount of line capacity—capacity which was, and still is, vitally necessary for the inter-city business and for increasingly high speed freight trains.

Present Situation

By the time that the effect of the 1968 Transport Act made itself felt, the rural network was a rather curious animal. It was—and still is—by no means negligible in size. The services now account for some 980 million passenger miles (1575 million km) a year which is 5% of the total passenger mileage and provide for all the traffic at some 500 stations out of a BR total of 2400. The revenue of £27.5 million represents some 5% of BR passenger revenue. Significantly, in 1974, the last year for which individual figures are available, they absorbed about £50 million, or 32% of the passenger network grant.

By this time, of course, the most truly rural services had been weeded out.

139

Remote rural termini like Laxfield, Suffolk or Newcastle Emlyn, Tollesbury or Pateley Bridge had long since gone. Those that remained were, for the most part, more defensible in social benefit, even if not in financial, terms. They can be characterized, perhaps, as belonging to one of the following groups:

(i) The 'survival of the fittest' class—those routes which, amongst a group or even an actual network of lines, survived as the strongest— or perhaps one should say the least weak economically. Norwich— Cromer—Sheringham might be taken as an example, the sole survivor apart from one private railway, of the formerly quite extensive network in north Norfolk.

(ii) Those which survived because of some peculiarity of geography—the Plymouth-Gunnislake service, for instance, which avoids a lengthy road detour to cross the Tamar valley.

(iii) Lengthy lines providing a service in remote, and mainly very thinly peopled areas. The Cambrian Coast line and the Kyle of Lochalsh route are typical.

(iv) Services on routes of significance for other purposes, passenger or freight, where it is operationally practicable and commercially reasonable for a service, which to some extent may perform an inter-urban function, to make in addition a number of stops of a rural character. The section of the Lincoln—Crewe service between Lincoln, Newark and Nottingham is a typical example.

Development and Improvement

After the 1968 Transport Act, with the total costs of the service covered by grant under the Cooper Brothers formula (9.1) it might perhaps be imagined that all incentive towards improvement of these services had disappeared. This, however, was very far from being the case. Grant levels were examined line by line by the Department of the Environment, and the threat of withdrawal of grant, leading to closure, was a real one. Closure was not a neutral situation for British Rail. Allocated, but none the less inescapable, costs, and the loss of contributory revenue, meant virtually always that British Rail was worse off from closure.

As a result, much attention has been paid to the development of traffic and the achievement of operating economies on these lines. For example, in 1973, a major marketing effort was launched to encourage travel on the Middles-brough–Whitby line, and carryings are now twice their 1972 level. This line carries commuters into Middlesbrough, serves several isolated rural communi-ties, and conveys holiday traffic to Whitby and the North Yorkshire Moors National Park. The first market has been stimulated by the opening of a new station at Gypsy Lane and the provision of a bus/rail feeder from Guisborough, the second by the introduction of a more frequent regular interval train service, and the third by publicity such as the 'Esk Valley Walkways' brochure, designed to encourage combined rail and walking tours.

Marketing drives have also been undertaken on other rural services, such as Hull–Scarborough, where combined rail and admission tickets to local attractions, and competitions for rail users, have increased traffic considerably. Long distance commuter traffic from the Bridlington and Driffield areas is being attracted into Hull, and the existence of the train service has encouraged the development of commuter villages such as Hutton Cranswick. In East Anglia, holiday runabout tickets have been made available at local council offices, and timetables and other promotional material have been widely distributed. Many other examples could be quoted of this kind of marketing activity.

The marketing effort was paralleled by a considerable and most welcome enthusiasm on the part of local authorities to seek solutions to their transport problems by supplementing the central grant.

Local authority finance has been provided for the Peterborough–Spalding passenger service, for example, and among the reopened stations are Ruskington and Metheringham, on the March–Doncaster line, and Magdalen Road on the Cambridge–King's Lynn line. In all, 18 stations have been reopened with financial assistance from local authorities since 1970, most of them in rural areas.

Figure 9.1 Diesel multiple-unit train as used by British Rail on many rural branch line services. A face-lift is being given to 2000 diesel multiple-unit vehicles to improve their standard of passenger amenity and comfort. The refurbished vehicles are being repainted in a new white and blue livery. This is the first unit to be refitted, a three car set built by Metro-Cammell in 1958.

The result of these combined efforts is a praiseworthy one,. In a field where public transport is in almost universal decline, the volume of traffic on 'other provincial services' remained more or less static at 1000 million passenger miles from 1970 to 1976, as did earnings, in real terms (about £26 million at 1976 price levels). Trends on individual services have varied widely, however, as Table 9.1 indicates.

TABLE 9.1   Comparative Statistics on 10 'other provincial services'

| | \multicolumn{3}{c}{Passenger miles/kilometres (millions)} | | |
	miles 1970	km	miles 1976	km
Shrewsbury-Aberystwyth	9.4	15.1	5.4	8.7
Preston-Barrow	22.5	36.2	21.4	34.4
Cardiff-Crewe	30.5	49.0	43.4	69.8
Bristol-Salisbury	8.6	13.8	8.8	14.1
Bristol-Weymouth	17.2	27.7	12.5	20.1
Glasgow-Oban	7.9	12.7	8.7	14.0
Darlington-Bishop Auckland	3.7	5.9	3.1	5.0
Leeds-Morecambe	24.2	38.9	21.8	35.1
Cleethorpes-New Holland/ Barton	5.1	8.2	4.0	6.4
Cambridge-Peterborough	7.7	12.4	10.2	16.4
	(136.8)	(220.0)	(139.3)	(224.0)

Coupled with the effort to generate revenue is the attack on costs. We have gone as far as we can in this direction. Most rural services are now operated by 'pay trains', and intermediate stations have become unstaffed, their passenger facilities reduced to a minimum. Track and signalling have been simplified, in some cases to the extent of 'one train on line' operation over a single track with no intermediate signalling or passing loops. We have also experimented in the past with lightweight rail vehicles; one of the main difficulties in developing this idea further is that a substantial build of such vehicles would be required to justify the high initial cost of design and development, whereas the number of services for which they would be suitable is limited. A further area for economy, particularly in the eastern counties, is the automation of level crossings, but the high capital cost of automatic half barriers, and their unsuitability for heavily used roads, again reduce the scope for action.

The 1974 Railways Act brought about a change in the method of grant aiding the railway passenger network. The principal change affecting rural services was the cessation of individual unremunerative service grants paid under S. 39 of the 1968 Transport Act, and the substitution of a new system of grant. Under Section 3 of the 1974 Act, the Minister is given the power to impose obligations on the board to operate passenger services, and is required to compensate the board for their provision in the form of a block grant, known as the Public Service Obligation Grant. This is paid in respect of the deficit on the passenger system as a whole, and is not calculated for each individual service. Under the new system, the allocation of infrastructure costs between passenger and freight services is based on the premise that the track and signalling are provided primarily for passenger trains, the latter receiving a correspondingly higher proportion of infrastructure cost than under the old method. The result of this change is that passenger services show a higher accounting deficit and receive a proportionally higher government grant.

One reason for the relative stability of traffic on rural services over the past few years is that they do not stand alone. They are important for local purposes but do not depend on this exclusively since they form an important adjunct to a growth business, namely, inter-city. This is illustrated by most of the following other provincial services, again chosen at random, whose contributory revenue (revenue attributable to the remainder of the network—principally inter-city—from journeys made only partly on the local service) is compared with the earnings from local journeys on the service itself:-

TABLE 9.2

	1975 Figures (£000s)	
	Local Earnings	*Contributory Revenue*
Hull-Scarborough	293	175
Ipswich-Lowestoft	192	60
Preston-Windermere	41	257
Barrow-Whitehaven-Carlisle	238	153
Carnforth-Crewe	590	657
Plymouth-Gunnislake	28	5
Glasgow-Oban	108	59
Edinburgh-North Berwick/Dunbar	36	1

Their continuing role in this respect was in considerable contrast to the road services which had replaced rail services in the Beeching round of closures. Without any grant system and oriented mainly to local needs rather than

L

143

connection with the trunk rail network, many of these 'substitute services' have disappeared. Even since 1968, about a third of the replacement bus services introduced as conditions of rail closure consents have disappeared altogether, and another third have been substantially modified.

Economic Realities

This history must not, however, blind us to the realities of the present day. I have said that in 1974 rural rail services cost the taxpayer about £50 million. Allowing for inflation, they now account for about one sixth of the current Public Service Obligation (PSO) grant, a figure out of all proportion to the use made of these services. But possibly more serious than this is the fact that heavy infrastructure renewals will soon become due on many of these rural routes, necessitating their closure on safety grounds if the money is not spent. Furthermore, many of the diesel multiple units running on these services are nearing the end of their useful life. Redeployment of locomotive hauled stock to replace them increases the cost of operation, and any 'cascade' of rolling stock requires the introduction of new vehicles somewhere on the system. The current estimated cost of a new three-car diesel multiple unit is in the region of £420 000; the simplest form of single unit rail vehicle is unlikely to cost less than £60 000. It is difficult to justify this level of expenditure on the traffic volumes handled by most rural services, even taken in isolation.

But in the real world it cannot be looked at in isolation. There are, for example investment ceilings—and here it should be recalled once again that investment in this context does not mean what it means to most businessmen, the provision of new productive capacity. What has to be found, within—or perhaps one should say beneath—the ceiling, is the resources required to renew existing assets as they wear out. If—as is certainly the case at present—the ceiling is too low to keep all of the system in existence, something must begin to give. What should it be? Not Inter-city, which can bestow social benefits and earn a commercial return at the same time. Not the other bulk traffic activities which are those for which rail is particularly suited. One is driven forcibly to the conclusion that if anything has to go, it must be the rural rail service.

I do not want to sound overdramatic. A process of withdrawal of rail services from rural areas can—indeed must—be a relatively slow and ordered one. There will be scope for the exception—in special circumstances. There will be—there must be—time to put our house in order. It is with this aspect of domestic economy that I now want to deal.

The failures—alleged and in considerable measure real—of past closures have, in my view, very little to do with the change of mode. Only rarely has road an inherent disadvantage in the rural situation. It has, in fact some very substantial advantages. The smaller vehicle, freedom from the scheduling limitations of single lines and junctions, the ability to penetrate the market square and detour to the village—all of these are real assets.

The criticism of bus substitution for rail comes under many headings, but the most important without any doubt are the uncertain life associated with a bus service compared with rail under a Public Service Obligation grant, the lack of coordination, of information, of provision for luggage and so on. These have nothing to do with the mode, everything to do with the *modus operandi*. The Board's proposals for meeting the imminent threat to rural rail services posed by public expenditure restrictions have already been widely publicised. What we have done so far is to look at the whole of the passenger network, identify its weakest parts, and estimate what the effect would be of withdrawing many of the non-urban local passenger services and replacing them by limited stop bus services with an assured future. First indications are that this could involve withdrawal of passenger services from up to 2,500 miles (4023 km) of the existing network, and cause a reduction in the PSO support payment of at least £25 million a year. The aim would be to replace the local trains by bus services provided under contract to BR and financed through PSO grant. Fares, timings and levels and quality of services would be specified by BR. Attention would be paid to good interchange facilities, adequate provision for passengers' luggage, and the use of vehicles suited to their particular task. The bus services would be protected against withdrawal by the statutory procedure applicable to rail closures. Replacement bus services would be provided only where they could offer a standard of service comparable to the railway at less cost.

An important aspect of the replacement bus services would be their treatment as an extension of the national rail network. I have already touched on the physical aspects of good interchange and coordination; the services would also be marketed as part of the national system.

Through booking facilities to rail served destinations would be introduced wherever feasible, and the services would be included in the national railway timetable and on maps and other publicity. The buses themselves, though provided under contract to BR by existing operators, would no doubt carry a distinctive livery or identifying feature demonstrating that they were an integral part of the rail system. This degree of integration into BR's own operations and marketing would give the services a perceived security which other replacement bus services have lacked.

Once rail has taken to the road in this way, of course, other questions begin to arise. If the solution is appropriate for the country town which still has a rail service—perhaps more or less by historical accident of the closure process—is it also appropriate for the town which lost its service ten years ago? What is the relationship with the stage carriage service? What is the relationship with the

145

express coach? These are questions that can only be looked at on an integrated area basis.

Implementation of these proposals would require legislation, and therefore government backing is essential. The idea of replacing heavily subsidized rail services by assured bus service was proposed in the government's Transport Policy Consultation Document, and supported in the Board's response to that document. The extent of local authority support of replacement bus services was probably overplayed in the response and the majority of these services is now foreseen as falling into what the British Railways Board called 'Category 2'—fully integrated with the rail system and financed by central government. The idea of extending these bus operations into existing non-rail served areas is also a more recent thought.

The Board's discussions with the Department of Transport continued and the subject formed part of the input to the 1977 Transport Policy White Paper. The White Paper proposes consultation between the Board, the local authorities and the government on future methods of financing and determining the cost effectiveness of local rail services.

This should surely be the gateway to a new era in a wide field of public transport. One of the most extraordinary features of the present scene seems to be that in the urban situation a total coordination of modes of transport is generally accepted as providing the most effective instrument in a situation where the private car is unacceptable in city centres. Outside, in inter-urban travel, and as inter-urban shades into rural, there seems to be a feeling that only if public transport operators are made to compete will they be kept on their toes.

But why? As every contributor has said, public transport operators are in fact faced with competition of gigantic, possibly of overpowering dimensions, from the private car. Is it not vital in these circumstances that we combine the strengths of road and rail? There are others that coordinate more effectively than we do—predominantly in Europe. There are some who coordinate less— in Canada and the US, for example. There can be no doubt where public transport provides the most effective challenge to the private car. Combined, road and rail can be more than twice as effective as they can be isolation.

Reference

9.1 The Cooper Brothers formula is the method of cost allocation used in the calculation of individual passenger service grants before the introduction of Public Service Obligation Grant under the 1974 Railways Act.

PART THREE DISCUSSION
Public Transport Operation in Rural Areas
Chairman: T.D. Wilson

R. BAKER (Hawker Siddeley Dynamics Ltd.)

Mr. Knight explained the process of deciding the annual budget for capital items, for maintenance and for revenue support. However, these are not separate items; all three are interlinked. Capital invested in a car park, for example, brings with it a need for maintenance and for revenue support of public transport because of the loss of patronage to the car. There are many examples of such interlinking. Mr. Knight stated that eight different abbreviated public transport networks were being prepared in Cheshire as options to contain the escalating demand for revenue support for the buses. We have had a 'Beeching' on rural railways and it seems that we are now to have a 'Beeching' on rural bus services. Considering that capital, maintenance and revenue support are all interlinked, should not a 'Beeching' on rural roads be considered instead of on the bus services?[1] The Transport Policies and Programmes are supposed to be based on such compromises.

J. DRIVER (South Yorkshire County Planning Committee)

Political decisions and the allocation of resources are not a matter for the local authority. Even within the government guidelines it is not permitted to oppose government policies to make local decisions. South Yorkshire made the decision that fares should be pegged, which resulted initially in threats to withold the transport supplementary grant, threats which were subsequently implemented. The next effect of this decision was a 2p precept on top of other commitments. The policy involved public participation in a particularly direct manner at the Spring 1977 county elections. Of the 1 300 000 population in South Yorkshire, approximately 300 000 live in rural areas. A draft Structure Plan has just been put to public participation with the bold statement 'fares will not be raised until 1986'. This plan has been costed and the planning committee are prepared to stand by the cost implications, but not without any grant

---

[1]Beeching Report ("The Reshaping of British Railways", Parts 1 & 2, British Railways Board, HMSO, 1963). The Beeching Report recommendations instigated considerable reduction in the railway network, especially in rural areas. – Ed.

support at all. This will have to be determined politically at a higher level.

The concessionary fare scheme operated in South Yorkshire is the simplest imaginable. Every man over 65 or woman over 60 has a free pass for travel outside peak hours. Every school child as a 2p fare for every 10p of normal low fares. The result last year was £¾ million extra revenue on the buses. Ridership is increasing and although some consider it is being increased by free travel, the extra revenue proves that fare paying passengers are also on the increase. In attracting passengers back to buses and persuading them to leave cars at home the environment is being improved. In the rural areas there is no intention of affecting car travel because it supplements the public service. Personal mobility is an essential part of the quality of life and the cost to the general public justifies the decision.

J. WICKS (Martin and Voorhees Associates)

Rural transport is such a wide subject that unless we continually remind ourselves of our objective to provide for human needs we will lose sight of it in the mass of detailed discussion. Conventional planning approaches are inappropriate in the case of rural transport; this does not mean merely advocating certain experiments, important though they may be, but a continuous appraisal of the purpose of mobility in the countryside. Consideration of even more than transport/land-use relationships is necessary. This consideration has to embrace the relationships between transport and lifestyle, and the opportunities for people to engage in various activities. These considerations have been implicit in much of the discussion. For example, they are central to the difference between the Oxfordshire and Bedfordshire approaches—but it is necessary to remind ourselves often of this particular aspect of rural transport.

Although many people accept the importance of determining the needs of dwellers in particular areas, the difficulty of doing so has been indicated. Some doubt has been expressed on how representative various bodies and pressure groups are, but if their nature is recognized and the real part they have to play, then the representativeness or otherwise of their structure is not important. In the work that Martin and Voorhees Associates has done in various rural areas, there has been no difficulty in contacting the inarticulate members of the community as long as a proper social research approach has been adopted. As Mr. Blowers pointed out, one can never ask simplistic questions such as 'What sort of service do you want?' because the respondent being unaware of the range of alternatives which are possible, is probably not able to judge what he wants.

The social psychologist is best to analyze the lifestyles, attitudes and needs of people in various communities and the transport planner to determine the appropriate services. The process is not a two-stage one; there has to be a complete partnership between the disciplines. This approach, although it includes working in and with local communities, does not rely on those communities to solve planners' problems for them. Professional planners, transport operators and decision makers cannot escape the responsibility to exercise their professional judgement. The possibility of using an approach such as the one described refutes the suggestion that county councils are too big to grasp the problem of local needs of rural dwellers. It is the way in which the interventionist approach to planning rural transport can be made possible.

v.a. KNIGHT (Cheshire County Council)

Mr. Baker is perhaps pre-judging the issue when he suggests there is to be a 'Beeching' on the bus services of Cheshire. The eight networks are primarily needed because if what was happening with projected demands for bus services was not examined against the increased demand for revenue support on the buses, there would indeed have been a 'Beeching' in Cheshire. Instead, eight levels of service are being looked at and related to the population affected. It could be that when the members see the effect of reducing revenue, they may want to give more support. This evaluation is being attempted to prevent precipitate arbitrary cuts. An arbitrary cut without knowledge of its effect on people would be the worst thing that could possibly happen. Such an evaluation was not made before the Beeching proposals where the effort was directed mainly towards reducing the cost of the service. It is recognized that if peak bus services are cancelled the cost of hiring buses for education will be increased, perhaps doubled. This is being examined and will be reported to members so that they can make a judgement.

It is true that building public car parks does have revenue effects, but such activity has virtually ceased. The policy is to try to increase the cost of town centre car parking, reduce the stay of cars in town centre car parks to attempt to get the short-stay shopper using the car park rather than the commuter. This may not be the right answer because it is the peak hour bus service that costs money. It might be better to fill the town centre car parks with cars that are there all day and use the off-peak buses for the shoppers and make a better overall use of buses. It is not the simple issue indicated. In Cheshire, effects are monitored and attempts are made to correct mistakes as they occur. By moving steadily in this direction it is possible to check that proposals are right.

D. AWDAS (Devon County Council)

All systems need to adapt with time and Devon are endeavouring to maintain a basic network. The frequencies are changing but because the network remains people still have mobility. This may not be as frequent or as regular a service as some would ideally like but it is sufficient to meet essential needs.

The abandoning of some roads is being looked into thoroughly in Devon.

149

Although not being the largest county, Devon has the greatest road mileage and attempts are being made to reduce it. The reduction will not be enormous, but will be step-by-step similar to the approach towards buses in Cheshire, attempting to find a reasonable solution without discarding something that might be needed in later years.

The county council is a big organization; it is in some ways remote from many rural dwellers. District councils are used to give some link between people and the county council itself. An Area Structure has been set up in Devon as a way of allowing the county council to try to get closer to the people. It would appear to be working as the latest rural transport experiments indicate, but perhaps there is still room for improvement.

V.A. KNIGHT

It is very often suggested that the number of roads can be reduced. In Cheshire, the possibility was investigated of not maintaining any road which led to a single farm or to fields, but this represented less than 0.05% of the roads. It is far cheaper to maintain a gravel road by surface dressing once every ten years than it is to have to repair pot holes. If the county council do not surface dress once every ten years, then the farmer will have to pay for filling in the pot holes.

R.P. KILVINGTON (Loughborough University of Technology)

Mr. Keen was correct to state that if rural rail services do have to be withdrawn, an integrated express bus service will be undoubtedly beneficial, especially if British Rail themselves are able to operate it so that they can provide a fully coordinated service with connecting bus services printed in the rail timetable! From research work carried out for the Welsh Council in rural Wales, it seems likely that the whole area would benefit from a good express bus service compared with the existing rail services.

What is disappointing, especially coming from a British Rail representative, is the presumed total abandonment by British Rail of the idea that any improvements can be made both in the existing operating characteristics and especially in the costs of rural rail operation. The British Rail rural network appears to be facing sacrifice simply because of overstaffing and its outmoded form of operation. In Pryke & Dodgson[2] and particularly in Volume Two of the Government Green Paper[3] which compares European Rail efficiency, British Rail is shown to perform particularly badly. Rather than looking at the bus as an alternative, British Rail should be looking at rural rail operation. In the rest

[2]PRYKE, R. & DODGSON, J. The Rail Problem—An Alternative Strategy', Martin Robertson, 1975.
[3]Transport Policy. HMSO, 1976.

150

of Europe, especially in Denmark, one-man operation (driver/ticket collector/ guard), lower accepted levels of maintenance and even safety standards abound; in short, fewer nineteenth-century operating criteria exist. By adapting such systems to the UK, better and cheaper rail services could be provided in the rural areas, which could benefit not only British Rail but also their passengers and indeed the general economy of the whole country.

There are usually two counter arguments to this approach. First, there is union pressure against reducing employment on the railways. British Rail have already done commendably well in reducing manning levels, but surely for employees half a railway is better than none and this is the alternative. Secondly, BR would need considerable levels of investment to effect significant changes in operating criteria. On the other hand, development of an express bus service will require considerable investment. There is scope for BR to acquire these resources and use the money in a different way.

R. BARRETT (Freeman Fox and Associates)

The British are rather isolated and introverted in their approach by not considering what is happening in other countries. In France, for example, there is a centralized economy run from Paris, there are no inter-city bus services, the municipalities either run their own bus services or have concession agreements and all rural transport is carried out by private operators. These private operators do not cost the municipalities or central government, any money to provide a service for the rural communities, albeit that in some areas the service is very poor.

In one island of the Seychelles, there is an excellent public transport system. 70% of the community live in rural areas and 85% of these people are served with buses with a frequency of less than 20 minutes and in certain areas, buses run at three minute intervals. This operates in a perfectly free enterprise system. The operators are all private and make money—a satisfactory system for all concerned.

In Britain, are we not constrained by an industry which had developed in an historical way? This existing industry is being used to tackle rural transport problems which, in fact, the industry was never designed to tackle. Would not a better service be provided by private operators running specific services according to the social needs in their area and with consequent financial savings both to local authority and central government?

R.C. EDWARDS (Norfolk County Council)

Mr. Keen mentioned that more progress seemed to be made in bus/rail coordination in urban areas and very little, or the opposite, in rural areas. Norfolk has a coordinated approach—it has identified what it considers the main corridors of public transport flow and has nominated a spine service in each one and indicated the intention of protecting the spine service from competition. Mr. Keen also indicated that the Beeching closure programme was stopped in mid-stream. Norfolk must be exceptional for not only was every line that Beeching recommended for closure closed, but three additional lines have been closed and demolished. In his suggestions for the replacement of railway services by express bus services, Mr. Keen refers to standards of service comparable to railway at less cost. Norfolk differs from most parts of the country by its position as a geographical extremity. It is a long way from the main transport trunk system of the country and the time factor between coach and rail, particularly of course, rail potential, must be taken into account when considering journeys of 80–100 miles (130-160 km) to the nearest main line railway point. In discussions about the protection of spine services, the National Bus Company say they are not competing with British Rail but are serving different markets. It is paradoxical that Mr. Keen says coaches can deal with the market being catered for by British Rail at present. A bus service with an assured future is a difficult concept to grasp and one would ask, who will continue to pay for such services if no-one uses them?

P.A. KEEN (British Railways Board)

In answer to Mr. Kilvington, an immense amount has been done in improving efficiency and cutting costs of rail services already. The majority of rural rail services are virtually unstaffed on the ground in terms of operating staffs. Engineering staffs have been cut. The 'pay train' system of operation is cheap and efficient. The stock that British Rail are using is not the most modern, but it happens as a result of provision for depreciation on a historical basis to be extremely economic for this purpose. There are areas where it looks as if further economies could be made particularly of course in areas like manned level crossings and in some sections of double track which obviously could be single. Mr. Kilvington did touch on one of the key factors when he said that enhanced services require capital. Resignalling is very expensive and when this is added to the ultimate cost of replacement of rolling stock, the comparison with the capital investment involved in road replacement services is unattractive. Denmark is committed to a policy of rail refurbishment on rural services, but the internal studies undertaken by DSB (Danish Railways) showed very clearly that this was economically a very much less attractive alternative than a road replacement. When discussing European experience in this context, the example of France chosen by Mr. Barrett is not a good example to take on the European Continent.

Mr. Edwards tied his points together by asking who pays for the service if nobody uses it? The short answer is hopefully no-one. In practise, we would see bus replacement services of this kind as forming part of the total public service obligation grant for British Rail and the services themselves having the same degree of certainty that applies to the national rail system. This does provide a certain degree of assurance, an assurance that would be increased of the value for money component in it was increased. There is, of course, always the Transport Users Consultative Committee (TUCC) procedure which seems to prevent BR doing things for an average of 156 weeks per case—a fairly long time for reflection.

Mr. Edwards made some very interesting comments on the question of distance. The calculation of how appropriate the bus is as substitution for rail is a complicated one in which distance is one of the very important factors. I would see the most likely possibilities falling very much in the short distance category—around 20 miles (32 km).

D. AWDAS

We should look at other people's experiences and try to learn something from them—even if at the end of the day we don't get very far with it.

Private operators are certainly essential in any rural county; they have a role to play, but they cannot take over the whole role of public transport in the rural areas. In our own experience, there are insufficient suitable operators; it can be argued that if there is demand, people will come in and fill the bill and supply the services you want. But in general terms they fill a complementary function. The National Bus Company with its ability to radiate throughout counties and across boundaries as well fulfils one role. The independent, particularly if it relates to contract work, fulfils another. These two types of operator combine together to produce the ideal answer.

D. HOLDING (Newcastle-on-Tyne Polytechnic)

Mr. Keen wants to see more coordination between operators in the Shire Counties. I would like to raise the question of a political decision of a different kind in a particular context. Crosville, an NBC company, introduced a limited-stop service between Chester and Manchester. The Traffic Commissioners granted the service, to which British Rail had objected. British Rail took the case to appeal and won. The Secretary of State has now instructed Crosville to take their service off again. What are the views of Cheshire and British Rail on this?

V.A. KNIGHT

Cheshire County Council supported Crosville on the basis that, although the train service from Chester to Manchester was losing money, the express bus service did not parallel the rail route and was giving access to people who would not, have not and never would use British Rail. The bus service formed a very good strategic route because the time by bus from Chester to Manchester was much greater than by rail and a great number of the passengers would not travel from one end of the route to the other. It was therefore supported on the basis that it was an additional facility for the public, which the Members thought was an advantage. British Rail opposed it because they thought that they would lose more than they would gain. Cheshire County Council thought that the people using public transport would gain more from having the bus service.

P.A. KEEN

Without knowing the details of the case—it must clearly be a disagreement on fact, in the sense that Cheshire thought that it would not abstract from BR, and BR thought that it would. Such a quasi-legalistic process is not the way to coordinate transport properly.

V.A. KNIGHT

Mr. Keen is correct, the legal process available is not the way to properly coordinate public transport. The Cheshire County Council were trying to look after the people who were going to be catered for by the service and judging from the amount of use that came from that service when it was put in, it was well used. The objection from British Rail came before the service was instigated. The council have been prepared to look at it after it had been started but the inquiry turned it down so the service has to be withdrawn. As a coordination process, it is a dismal failure and, in the end, the user is the loser.

R.C. WINFIELD (Dyfed County Council)

Dyfed County Council covers an area which has the benefit of three rural rail services. In each case, for the majority of rail journeys, it is necessary to change at Shrewsbury or Swansea, as the services are essentially feeder services rather than part of the nationwide system. Rail services, without question, provide an infinitely better service in terms of comfort as well as speed than any present day coach service. For psychological and historical reasons, there is a much wider market for rail services than there ever will be for buses, particularly in the more middle-class areas. Thirdly, in the area, the political importance of railways is very evident. These attitudes cannot necessarily be identified scientifically, but the people who make the decisions do care very strongly for their railways. It has also become quite obvious when rail closure is threatened that there is a complete lack of trust between the politicians, pressure groups and British Rail. Perhaps British Rail or the Government should take steps to investigate before such services come up for renewal of stock, the possibility of down-grading them to light railways. On a long tour in Switzerland, we seemed continuously to be changing from one form of transport to another, but this proved no disadvantage because the system was fully integrated—light railways and heavy railways, cable railways and ferries—interchanges from one side of the platform to another with no more than two or three minutes wait. No inconvenience was caused in changing between light and heavy rail systems.

DR. A. OCHOJNA (Greater Glasgow Passenger Transport Executive)

The approach that the Transport Executive is trying to adopt in Strathclyde towards rural transport shows up some of the advantages and disadvantages of the Scottish regional system which combines Shire Counties and Metropolitan Counties. One disadvantage is the large number of transport operators including two major ferry operators, five Scottish bus group subsidiaries, 40 independent operators and a Passenger Transport Executive. In addition, there are two British Rail networks, an underground and internal air services to the islands. To cope with this, there are five area coordinators and a chief transport coordinator. There are two advantages of size—one is operational and the other is political. From an operational point of view, there is a very big basic network completely within the region. The political advantage is the need to make the region be aware and demonstrate clearly that its money is not being funnelled into Glasgow and to ensure the rural area is seen to be getting a fair deal. In transport terms this means that we are not developing a rural transport policy or an urban transport policy but we are expected, in the case of subsidy, to talk about the regional transport policy. Our network has been studied and an index system produced for all the villages in the region. The reason for doing this was basically to identify those areas requiring special consideration. As a result, 9 small areas have been found with problems. These areas tend to lie off the basic network. On the basis of a village index of need, subsidy can be allocated fairly over these areas. In Strathclyde, the tendency is to leave to the politician the decision on the split of financial allocation between the urban and the rural areas. Within the smaller areas the tendency will be for local opinion, gauged by Transport coordinators, to decide how local subsidy is best spent. Obviously, the level of service for one area will be different from that for another. It must be realized that simply to be remote does not necessarily justify extra subsidy. This intended approach is based on a realization that subsidy and its allocation is the critically sensitive issue.

P.A. KEEN

Mr. Winfield from Dyfed complains that the British Rail Board do not seem to take much notice of the Central Wales lines. The Board's policy in respect of rural lines is to delegate a great deal of authority and initiative related to promoting them, to local managers. This certainly pays and publicity gimmicks such as cheap fares and slogans and as the fairly powerful 'use it or lose it'

155

have had results. It is an inevitable consequence of delegating authority locally that results are unequal. People approach things in different ways and conditions are different, and local initiative is important.

The Swiss system is admirable, but the cost of modern railway rolling stock in Switzerland is fantastic. Secondly, and much more relevant in this context, is the control of local transport operations almost wholly by the Cantons. In the UK most of the rural services are covered by central grant not local grant. The result is that decisions have to be taken in relation to national resources. Although someone is bound to be the loser, the existing system does provide the opportunity for counties to contribute where they think there is a particular political requirement. Spalding/Peterborough for example was an example of a rail service maintained as a result of grant from a shire county. Such a solution is open to Dyfed.

D. AWDAS

Strathclyde seem to be operating under a different system from the one Devon are expected to operate under. Nevertheless the first decision is still an urban/rural split and problem areas are taken to one side and dealt with separately. Most of the shire counties in England are probably tackling the problem in a similar manner. There is obviously a far greater task of coordination in Strathclyde because of the size of the area and the number of operators within it.

DR. V. BONO (ATAN-FORMEZ Project for Public Transport Managers School, Italy)

FORMEZ is a private management consultancy firm dealing principally with social and economic matters. It is about to enter the transport field with the opening of a school for public transport managers in Italy. Two difficulties which influence Italian transport policy are orientation towards new priorities in harmony with the economic development of the community and secondly, avoiding the suffocation of increasing motor traffic and the other factors upon which the country's economy depends.

ATAN is already the leading transport company in Campania and will develop in the whole of the south of Italy. Consequently, rapid expansion and the demand for services brings about the need to rely on more advanced administrative models and policies which will allow the best use of resources. The development of these new administrative policies and the introduction of different organizational models cannot be carried out without effective training of the bus company management staff.

Considering the size and importance of ATAN, the decision to furnish the company with a new internal structure is decisive. The request made to

FORMEZ for collaboration and technical assistance comes within the scope of the FORMEZ management centre. We are dealing, in effect, with the development of a formative structure in the policy field of a company tightly linked to local administration and operating in a sector of primary social need.

ATAN will only be satisfied with a complex plan which will link the company's internal organizational needs to the social and economic development contexts of the territory in which the bus services are running, and to a specific formative and research programme.

PART FOUR
New Rural Transport Techniques

CHAPTER TEN

Rural Bus Services— An Assessment of Current Experiments

D.W. Glassborow

Economic Background

In 1954 I was chosen to create and take charge of the economics division of the British Transport Commission. When that useful body was dispersed by the Transport Act 1962, I had a similar role with the Railways Board, until given the opportunity to join the Transport Holding Company. With the regrettable, regretted and unnecessary killing of that successful public enterprise by the Transport Act 1968, I found myself in the National Bus Company. Among my initial tasks was that of formulating a policy for dealing with the specific provisions of that Act in relation to rural bus services, which are mainly contained in Section 34—'Assistance for rural bus or ferry services' and Section 54—'Railway closures'.

There was, also, a strong link between these matters and the application of the principles of Cmnd 3437—'Nationalized Industries—A Review of Economic and Financial Objectives' to an assessment of a financial target for NBC consistent with the financial duties specified in Section 41 of the Transport Act 1968.

To carry out this task in the manner officially so prescribed, the surplus required by Section 41 in all its rigour would first have to have been calculated and the figure so obtained been reduced by the aggregate annual losses on services provided to meet the social needs of more or less isolated communities and supported by the traditional system of cross-subsidization.

The cost of assessing the losses on all such individual services was clearly immense. It would also have taken a very long time. It would have given immense scope for fruitless argument, since any system of route costing involves the arbitrary apportionment of costs common to a number of, in some cases all of, the routes of an individual undertaking.

161

We should remind ourselves that the NBC is not the bus industry. The requirement to give NBC a financial target was met by an entirely practical and commonsense decision to determine it by the exercise of judgement. This had its counterpart in the decision generally to continue with cross-subsidization as a means of maintaining the network of bus services. In the late 1960s and early 1970s subsidies were provided to bus passengers by relieving bus operators of the costs of having the roads provided, with first the partial and then the complete rebate of fuel duty, and of part of the costs of providing vehicles with the introduction of the bus grant at 25% and its increase to 50%.

We thus had a situation in which general support for bus operators was provided to keep in being unremunerative bus services which were not precisely identified. On the other hand direct subsidies were provided for 'unremunerative' railway passenger services on a costing formula which provided, in fact, a balance of cash to support railway services in general.

It could not last. These sources of financial support became inadequate to keep the rail networks and the bus networks in being. So the railways were given general financial support. The means to keep bus services in being moved in the opposite direction to financial support for specific services, through the powers given to local authorities to obtain taxpayers' money for this purpose. The flexibility of the Government's approach is further emphasized by the arrangement by which metropolitan counties provide specific taxpayers' support to local railway services through the Passenger Transport Executives. This chapter will consider the utility of current experiments. The measure of their utility is their contribution to the solution of the growing financial problem of providing public transport services. This is no longer a matter of how to support bus services in fringe areas. The main networks of bus services between and into cities, towns and large villages are now beginning to slide into unprofitability.

The problem of providing and operating outside built-up areas is quite simply one of finding the money. There is, in general, no technical problem involved—though some routes in a few areas cannot take standard size buses. The problem being a financial one, the objective of policy in this area must be value for money, the provision of a given quality of service at the minimum cost to the taxpayer and ratepayer. Each experiment should test which of a choice of ways of operating a service provides the highest ratio of passenger revenue to total cost, subject to a given maximum loss. Not operating at all requires no subsidy from the taxpayer and ratepayer, so there is an obvious need for specifying a maximum sum of money or a minimum level of service to be provided, before any experiment is begun.

Even this takes us only a little way towards solving the long term problem. It is sensible to experiment to try and find out if the present level of service could be provided more cheaply, or if the present loss could support a higher level of service than is the case at present. A fundamental difficulty, however, is that alternative ways of providing a public transport service are seldom, if ever, close substitutes. Comparisons between systems should therefore include an evaluation in money terms of the ways in which one system provides better or worse services, as well as assessing the difference in costs after crediting passenger revenue. What might appear at first sight to be a simple financial exercise can therefore turn out, in theory at least, to require a complex socio-economic investigation.

It has been necessary to make these introductory points at some length because, from my own study of the literature and from the pronouncements of many people outside the public transport business, there appears a widespread belief that the experimental services will not only be better but will save expense. Very often this is not the case.

Elements of Public Transport Cost

The main elements in the cost of providing a public transport service are:–

(i) The driver.
(ii) The staff employed to enable the vehicle to be put on the road at the right time, in the right place and in the right condition, to bring the existence of the service to the notice of the travelling public and to handle the money which is collected from the public.
(iii) Buying the vehicle and the parts and materials needed for its maintenance.
(iv) Fuel.
(v) The roads and the terminal facilities.

Types of Experiments

The various experiments can be classified into types, according to their cost-reducing characteristics, if any:–

(a) Those where the cost of the driver and other staff is reduced or eliminated.
(b) Those where the cost of the driver and vehicle is mainly charged to other people.
(c) Those where the vehicle ceases to operate to a predetermined time-table, the so called demand-responsive systems, with the aim of reducing uneconomic mileage or improving load factors.

Examples of the first kind involve the use of volunteer drivers. Two cases in this country are well-known—the community bus schemes, such as the Norfolk and Clywd Village Bus Service (Figs. 10.1, 10.2) and the social car schemes, of

163

Figure 10.1   Norfolk community bus. A Ford Transit minibus operated jointly by the Eastern Counties Omnibus Company Ltd and Norfolk County Council with volunteer drivers (Commercial Motor)

Figure 10.2   Clwyd community bus. Special bodied Ford Transit operated jointly by Crosville Motor Services Ltd and Clwyd County Council (Crosville Motor Services Ltd)

which that at Bridgnorth was probably the first. There are significant differences. The community bus operates under a permit issued under Section 30 of the Transport Act 1968, instead of a stage-carriage licence, but qualifies for rebate of fuel duty and bus grant. Fares are collected from the passengers.

Social cars schemes are an alternative to taxis or hire cars. They are not available to all who might wish to use them and, in consequence, cannot really be regarded as belonging to the public transport sector. They function as part of the social welfare system. The costs to the community seem remarkably high.

Some recent figures (at the time of writing) for the Village Bus and a social car scheme are of interest:-

	Village Bus £	*Social Car Service* £
Cost per vehicle mile	0.06	0.06
Cost per passenger journey	0.27	1.25
Revenue per passenger journey	0.27	NIL

These figures underline the difference between the community bus service and the social car scheme, in cost to the community as well as in function. Indeed the only thing they usually have in common is that the driver is a volunteer.

There were, initially, heavy costs—at least heavy in relation to the volume of service provided—of training drivers for the Norfolk Village service. The above cost figures include a contribution towards re-couping those costs. It seems, therefore, that where the conditions are right, (and these have been set out in a contribution to the TRRL Symposium on Unconventional Bus Services) community bus services can provide a useful fringe service to the main extra-urban public transport system, at a minimum cost to public funds. By the criterion of cost per passenger or per passenger mile falling on public funds, they seem to rank very highly. But they cannot be an alternative to that main system.

Turning next to the public transport service which rides on the back of another, we have two main possibilities—the post bus and the school bus (Fig. 10.3). The post bus, as it is now being developed in this country, has nothing or almost nothing in common with the network of unprofitable bus services to be found in some countries, where a conventional bus operation has developed from mail-carrying horse-drawn coach services which also carried passengers. Services of that kind are now usually an embarrassment, a financial burden, to the postal administrations concerned, who cannot afford to support them from the falling net revenues of letter and parcel posts.

165

Figure 10.3 Commer/Dodge Royal Mail post bus operated by the Post Office in rural areas (Commercial Motor)

The post bus services in this country which are now being developed, principally in Scotland, are rarely suitable for school children and for travel to and from work. They are simply services which carry passengers on vehicles used for delivery and collection of mail. The journey is of a reasonable speed when the mail is being collected to bring it to the sorting centres in the town. It is very slow when the postman is delivering to individual houses. From the Post Office viewpoint, there can be considerable financial benefit, because the use of the vehicle qualifies for fuel duty rebate and the special vehicle gets the bus grant. The service is run on a permit issued by the Traffic Commissioners. Thus the Post Office receives additional revenue, the fares paid by the passenger, and, in most instances, the purchase and running costs of vehicles (after bus grant and fuel duty rebate) suited to carrying passengers is not greater (and may be less) than the same costs for the postal services they are, in any case, required to run. The financial cost to the community, however, may show a less favourable picture, but published data do not reveal where the balance lies.

Another example is the use of school buses to carry fare-paying passengers. The passengers must want to travel at the times the children are going to and returning from school and over a route not served by a bus service. Either such a facility will benefit very few people or the school bus could be replaced by a normal bus service as part of the public transport network for the area. In terms of cost to public funds, a school bus carrying some adult passengers is no different from the same service operated under a stage carriage licence, except perhaps that the standards of safety may be lower and this may reduce the cost to the education authority.

In most cases of the third class of service, the demand-responsive operations, the experiments have been carried out in urban areas, where the financial prospects were the most promising. The prospect of devising highly ingenious systems of vehicle routeing using computer models has attracted some advocates of these experiments, while the idea that the use of small vehicles would save a lot of money has attracted other enthusiasts. In the event it appears that the dial-a-ride services have mainly been used by regular customers requiring almost a time-tabled basic service, with the variable operations responding to an irregular pattern tending to be a smaller part of the whole operation. Another feature has been the need to have an efficient data-recording system, so that phone-calls are properly logged and the necessary information for despatching a service easily retrieved. Even in the most favourable examples, revenue has seldom reached or exceeded thirty percent of the costs. More typical has been a figure of fifteen to twenty percent. My own feeling is that break-even can scarcely be achieved at fares much below the taxi level—and the quality of service is never going to reach the taxi level.

By 1977, there had not been any examples of rural dial-a-ride, but the very heavy cost to public funds per passenger in urban areas hardly suggests a better outcome in rural areas. It may be that a system by which people notify their general needs two days or more in advance and are then told when and where they will be picked up and also when their return journey will take place could be introduced. It is doubtful whether, in remote country areas, it would be possible to provide a dial-a-bus service on the same day as the 'phone call, even with two or three hours' notice.

Figure 10.4   Ford/Alexander midi-bus used by Eastern Counties Omnibus Company Ltd on rural services (Commercial Motor)

167

Some ideas have been developed for modifying an ordinary bus service to have some short-term demand responsive aspects. One of these currently being tested is the provision of an evening service from a large country town to a number of villages served during the day by two or more bus services. The bus is routed by the driver to set down passengers at any point on a number of specified roads, as required by the passengers. There are thus savings in bus and crew costs, compared with operating a last service on each of the day-time bus routes and unnecessary slow running by adhering to a day-time schedule is also avoided. At the time of writing figures are not available for this experiment.

Another idea, that of diverting, given advance notification, from a main route between two towns, to pick up and set down passengers in villages near to the route has not to my knowledge been tried. However, many potentially good direct services are already modified by scheduled diversions of this kind, so that they are made much slower and in consequence more expensive, and of inadequate quality to attract passengers who might travel on a direct service. A desk study of such a service was reported at the TRRL Symposium on Unconventional Bus Services. This related to a route which appeared more than normally favourable for such a service. What is not known is how many passengers would be lost from a direct scheduled service by slowing it down and creating uncertainty for all users about journey times, and, for some, about waiting times at intermediate pick-up points. What initially appeared an interesting idea on further examination appeared much less likely to be valuable. In relation to the main problem of public transport outside towns, the direction of current thought often seems to have an analogy with Nero's fire-fighting activities.

CHAPTER ELEVEN

Government Rural Transport Experiments 1977

D.C. Milefanti

The chapter sets out the range of issues the Government's rural transport experiments are designed to explore, so as to provide a basis for detailed advice to those interested in tackling the lack of services in a particular area, and also inform future government policy and general legislation.

It also sketches in the background to the experiments and the administrative arrangements for involving a wide range of interests in the programme; the method of approach used in setting up a balanced programme of 16 experiments in the four areas selected; the kind of services that are being established, either with or without the special legislation; and problems of subsequent assessment.

Four rural areas of about district scale were studied to find where in those areas there was a need for improved passenger transport. Next a look was taken at the existing orthodox bus services, to see whether they could be significantly improved within the same level of resources. Thirdly it was considered what 'unconventional' services might fill the gaps. The choice of unconventional services was made simply on what seemed best for the particular case being considered, disregarding the limitations of PSV licensing law. At the same time a Parliamentary Bill (11.1) was going through Parliament to make it possible for operations to be undertaken in selected experimental areas outside the general licensing law. Once the decision of principle had been made to undertake experiments in particular parts of the wider areas, household surveys were undertaken in order to ascertain the existing travel patterns of people living in the area, and their own perception of what other facilities they needed.

The experiments are intended basically to provide information relevant to changes in the statutory bus licensing system; and to provide the basis for 'do it yourself' advice to organizers of similar kinds of service. In rather greater detail, it is hoped that in the course of the experiments light will be thrown on:

(i) methods of getting better value out of existing orthodox bus services for the same use of resources;

(ii) methods of choosing a particular unconventional scheme for a particular area;

(iii) the variety of individual travel patterns at present, both in car-owning households and others;

(iv) what use is made of the various unconventional services, how satisfactory people find them, and how they affect travel patterns;

(v) the relationship between the transport needs of a particular area as seen by parish councils, women's institutes etc; those needs as seen by the individual respondent in advance of new services being introduced; and the actual use people make of a service once it is introduced;

(vi) ways of organizing and financing various kinds of unconventional services in a variety of circumstances;

(vii) circumstances in which the first choice of unconventional scheme is one which lies outside the pre-existing licensing law;

(viii) the value and any side effects of unconventional services which were excluded from pre-existing law.

This is a wide range of results to hope for from one programme, and it is clear that in practice more light will be thrown on some issues than on others, but the programme will also certainly provide a substantial basis for detailed advice to those interested in tackling the lack of services in a particular area, and also give a sound factual basis to future government policy and legislation. Indeed the results of the initial—preparatory—stages of the research were fed into the decision-making which led to the proposals for legislative change in the Transport Policy White Paper (11.2).

Those involved in the experiments are the Department of Transport; Welsh Office; Scottish Development Department; TRRL, who are actually conducting the experiments in England on behalf of the Department of Transport; and the people who sit on the central Steering Committee and four local working groups: both sides of the bus industry, taxi operators, the local authorities, Clerks of Traffic Commissioners, and the voluntary and consumer interest: the National Council of Social Service, the National Consumer Council, and the WRVS on the Steering Committee. The local working groups mirror this wide spread of interest with on the consumer side the women's institutes and local WRVS, Scottish and Welsh consumer councils, the Scottish Council of Social Service, the Transport Users Consultative Committee for Wales, in Yorkshire the Parish Councils Association and in Devon the community council.

Background to the Experiments

When the present government took office in February 1974 they were not satisfied that their predecessors' proposals to relax bus licensing in rural areas, embodied in the 1973 Road Traffic Bill, were the correct way to tackle rural transport problems. They felt that it was vital, before making any major change to legislation, to consult with all interested bodies both about the implications of such a change and about possible alternative methods of improving rural public transport. Neil Carmichael MP, then a junior minister at the Department of the Environment, therefore held a series of discussions with trade unions, bus operators, local authorities and other organizations involved in local passenger transport.

A number of significant points emerged from Mr Carmichael's study. There was obviously no consensus on the right way of tackling rural transport problems. The problems themselves differed in both nature and scale from area to area; there was clearly no single solution that could be shown to be acceptable throughout the country. Across-the-board changes in PSV licensing law of the kind that had been proposed, might produce benefits in areas with no public transport services remaining; in other areas their effect could be to kill off services which were still managing to survive. Whatever might take the place of conventional services that were withdrawn, there would be no guarantee of continuity or stability and the last state could be worse than the first.

On the other hand, although various alternatives to conventional stage carriage services had been, and were being, tried out in various parts of the country, no systematic effort seemed to have been made to exploit to the full the considerable scope for flexibility in the provision of services which already existed within the licensing system. What appeared to be needed therefore was a range of solutions which could be matched to the circumstances of particular areas.

The conclusions of the study were announced in the House of Commons in December 1975 by Dr John Gilbert MP, then Minister for Transport. He explained that in view of the fact that there was no general agreement about the extent to which changes in the licensing system would improve rural transport provision, a number of experimental schemes would be promoted in three or four areas of Great Britain to test ways of helping rural communities both within the existing public service vehicle licensing code, and under the terms of a short Bill, to be introduced when the opportunity arose, which would provide a modest relaxation of licensing for a limited period within the areas of the schemes.

The experimental projects would be the responsibility of local working groups, with representation from the local authorities, the bus operators, the unions and other bodies concerned. These groups would act under the general guidance of a steering committee embracing similar representation.

171

After further discussion with the various interests concerned, the Steering Committee was set up, and met for the first time in June 1976, under the chairmanship of Ken Marks MP, Parliamentary Under-Secretary of State at the Department of the Environment. With the creation of a separate Department of Transport, John Horam MP, Parliamentary Under-Secretary of State there, became Chairman.

Planning of the Experiments

The Government had decided to concentrate resources on a number of experiments divided between four areas: one each in Scotland and Wales and two in different parts of England. The first task of the Steering Committee, as the coordinating body for the experiments, was therefore to select the four areas so that they would between them be so far as possible representative of the really rural parts of Great Britain as a whole (excluding urban fringes and rural areas with an untypical density of population). Typicality was of course vital if the results of the experiments were to be applicable to rural areas generally—the main aim of the programme—and the inclusion of an urban fringe element would have added too much to the variables. Even within these constraints there were a fair number of suitable and eager counties. Choice was not easy, but after a great deal of consideration the committee decided that areas in Devon, North Yorkshire, South Ayrshire, in the Strathclyde region, and Dinefwr in the county of Dyfed would present a suitable diversity of conditions.

Following this decision, the local working groups were set up in each of these areas. At their first meetings, which took place in autumn 1976, they defined more precise areas which they felt from their own personal knowledge of local transport provision and problems would be suitable for the experiments. The areas they selected–and which were endorsed by the Steering Committee were:

    (i) Devon—Tiverton District and the former South Molton Rural District;

    (ii) North Yorkshire—the northern part of Harrogate District (excluding Harrogate itself, but including Ripon) together with the western part of Hambleton District and the former Leyburn Rural District;

    (iii) South Ayrshire—the southern parts of the districts of Cumnock and Doon Valley and Kyle and Carrick; (this area was later extended to include the district of Lanark);

    (iv) Dyfed—the northern part of the district of Dinefwr.

Once the study areas had been defined the next step was to make an assessment of travel needs and identify suitable sites within them for experimental schemes. Discussions were held with individuals and organizations, both on and off the working groups, to find out where there was unsatisfied transport demand.

172

With this information available the working groups were able to devise suitable schemes for the sites they had identified, and put proposals for these schemes to the Steering Committee.

Here there was a possibility of running into a problem of fit. For the programme to be effective the experiments needed to be chosen to meet the requirements of the area. This seemed a more straightforward approach, and nearer to the problems of ordinary schemes, than to draw up a shopping list of methods and seek sites where each method would suit. But it could conceivably have resulted in proposals for say a dozen WRVS social car schemes and nothing else.

This clearly would not have done: some duplication was desirable, to check on the conclusions from each, and to help bring out the way in which one general approach would need to differ in detail in different circumstances, and perhaps perform better in one context than in another. But at the same time it was desirable—within the constraint of the total number of schemes that could be duplicated—to test a fair variety of different types of service.

In the event however this worked out very well: the proposals put forward by the working groups, and endorsed by the Steering Committee in the Spring of 1977, covered a considerable range of different types of service but at the same time had a certain amount of necessary duplication. 16 schemes were approved, as follows:

   (i) two flexible-route services using small professionally-driven buses and offering pick-up on demand;

  (ii) a volunteer-driven community minibus, also with flexible routeing;

 (iii) three variants on a new form of operation involving shared hire-cars charging each passenger separately, at rates comparable to bus fares: these will provide highly flexible, low capital cost feeder services to local centres, longer distance bus services and (in Devon) local rail services;

 (iv) four schemes involving use of private cars to provide an organized transport service, authorized to charge fares, in areas of very low demand for public transport;

  (v) two hospital transport schemes, which (according to local need) may involve hire-cars, private cars or minibuses, to tackle the problems of people living in remote areas who need to get to centralized hospitals in towns, to visit patients or attend clinics;

 (vi) three post-bus services (one linked to one of the flexible-route minibus schemes): this is a familar concept in parts of Britain but needs further development and wider application;

 (vii) an emergency car service, catering for unexpected and urgent transport needs.

173

In addition a special zone is being designated in the Devon study area, where motorists will be able to make private arrangements to give lifts for payment. (This is illegal now if done on a regular basis.) Motorists in this zone will have to make sure that their insurance cover is valid. It is also being considered whether another lift-giving scheme can be added to the programme at a later stage.

In greater detail the 16 schemes are as follows:

Devon Study Area (four schemes)

(i) Shared hire-cars operating feeder services to local centres and to longer distance bus services and the Exeter-Barnstaple railway in a 15 mile (24 km) long zone stretching between Zeal Monachorum and Down St Mary in the South to Umberleigh and Chittlehampton in the north.

(ii) A feeder service using private cars authorized to charge fares, taking people to South Molton and possibly Dulverton from villages lying between those two towns (North Molton, Twitchen, Molland, West and East Anstey).

(iii) A community minibus, driven by fully-trained volunteers, taking people from an area north west of Tiverton into the town. The operating area would take in the parishes of Rackenford, Oakford, Stoodleigh, Loxbeare and Washfield.

(iv) A special zone designated under the Experimental Areas Bill where motorists would be authorized to make private arrangements to give lifts for payment on a regular basis provided there was no public advertisement. The zone will comprise the parishes of Washford Pyne, Puddington, Woolfardis-worthy, Kennerleigh, Poughill, Stockleigh English, Cheriton Fitzpaine, Cade-leigh, Cadbury and Stockleigh Pomery which occupy an area between Tiverton to the north east and Crediton to the south west. A local publicity campaign will be mounted to give motorists in the zone full details. The compulsory passenger insurance law will not be relaxed, and motorists in the special zone will have to make sure their cover would not be invalidated by acceptance of payments.

North Yorkshire Study Area (five schemes)

(i) A variable-route, pre-bookable, professionally driven bus service to Ripon, providing garden-gate pick-up and set-down facilities for people living in an area about 4 sq. miles (10.5 km²) lying west of the town. The villages of Galphay, Winksley, Grantley, Aldfield, Studley Roger, Fountains Bridge (near Fountains Abbey) will be among those served.

(ii) A shared hire-car service taking people from Colsterdale and villages further down the River Burn valley west of Masham, into the town of Masham for shopping, business and bus connections.

(iii) A hospital transport scheme to provide a way for those in remote places to get to hospitals in Northallerton. A survey has been carried out among visitors and out-patients. The results of this survey are now being analyzed and it is hoped shortly to announce the details of the proposed service.

(iv) A scheme using private cars authorized to charge fares, giving the villages of Hornby, Hackforth and Langthorne easier access to facilities in Old Catterick and Bedale, and access to long-distance coaches at Leeming Bar.

(v) Another private car scheme, serving four parishes to the north west of Northallerton. Villages served will include Danby Wiske, Kiplin and Great Langton, with journeys to Northallerton.

Scottish Study Area (four schemes)

(i) A hospital transport scheme giving representative rural zones of South Ayrshire a direct link to five major hospitals (three near Ayr, one at Irvine and one at Ballochmyle). Surveys among out-patients and visitors will be carried out before the scheme is implemented.

(ii) A shared hire-car service, serving a sparesely populated area around and to the east of the village of Stair, taking people to nearby towns—possibly Tarbolton and Mauchline—for shopping, business and bus connections.

(iii) A link between Dalmellington and Cumnock via Dalleagles. This will give the country area traversed better access to facilities in the two terminal towns, including district council offices near Cumnock.

(iv) A variable-route professionally driven minibus operating in the Carnwath-Dolphinton-Biggar area, providing connections with longer distance buses (e.g. to Lanark, Edinburgh) and linked with a post bus route from Biggar to Lanark via Quothquan and Pettinain.

Welsh Study Area (three schemes)

(i) A scheme involving private cars authorized to charge fares, serving the communities of Llangadog, Llanddeusant, Myddfai and Llandingat-Without and the town of Llandovery.

(ii) A voluntary emergency car service, operating throughout the study area, to meet urgent transport needs (e.g. hospital visits) for people who have no other means of transport.

(iii) A post bus operating in the upper valley of the Afon Tywi, north of Llandovery, and south towards Myddfai.

In addition, spare capacity in the local passenger vehicle fleet will be used to augment and balance the experimental services in the Welsh Study Area, and four school bus services are to be opened to the general public.

Of these schemes it is clear that 8 will fall outside the general licensing law and need to be authorized under the Experimental Areas Act. A further 3 may also need to rely on that Act according to precisely how the scheme evolves.

Evaluation and Experience

There are several methods of assessing the results of the experiments. The most immediate indicator is public use of the new services. Beyond this there is public comment on these services. Whilst this latter is not always a wholly reliable indicator (the dissatisfied are usually more vocal than the satisfied) it cannot be ignored. The increase—or decrease—in the number of passengers carried by orthodox public transport is also a guide to the effectiveness of the new services and together with figures on the use of those new services can be used in conjunction with financial statistics as a crude measure of value for money. Where it seems as though a drastic change has taken place in the travel patterns of people in the locality it may be necessary to hold a further full household survey. It is probable however that for most cases such a second survey would not be worthwhile, although it will clearly be necessary in the case of the area for general authorization of car-sharing, where there is no other way of measuring the effectiveness of the change.

While it is relatively straightforward to *measure* the effects of a new transport system, *evaluation* of them is much more difficult. The principal problem is that there is no generally agreed set of values to ascribe to the various benefits (or disbenefits) that may ensure. An obvious example of this type of disagreement is the value of time saved by passengers. The value which has been adopted by the Department of the Environment (and now the Department of Transport) as appropriate for evaluating road and urban transport schemes cannot necessarily be directly translated to rural passenger transport. Furthermore, where transport facilities are limited, the saving of travel/time on journeys which had already been possible may not be the main benefit of improved public transport: enhanced mobility and access to destinations otherwise difficult to reach may be of much greater importance. There are undoubted benefits attached to greater choice of shops (or frequency with which they may be visited), medical centres or even places of work, and the opportunities for the elderly or disabled to 'get out and about'. Such benefits cannot, however be readily quantified and if the various experimental transport options are to be subjected to the normal process of cost benefit analysis it will be necessary to establish a common set of values. This would be an ambitious and time-consuming task which would be outside the scope of our programme. Assessment of the benefits of local transport services is arguably, in any given case, largely a matter for the local authorities concerned under their statutory duties for transport coordination.

As a cost-benefit approach appears to be fraught with difficulties it may be possible to substitute for it a more pragmatic one. This is to establish a scale of effectiveness of public transport in rural areas. This might include such factors as the proportion of the population with bus access to convenient shops, the frequency of service etc. Such a scale, which would be partly descriptive, should be based, as far as possible, on the results of current research, but some arbitrary decisions would be unavoidable. Having established a scale, it will then be possible to examine the various public transport options proposed for an area, and identify those which, for the same cost, are most effective.

This alternative approach is not without its difficulties; the problem of establishing values is replaced by that of constructing a scale which will contain implicit value judgements. Furthermore, levels of performance which may be achieved at modest cost in some rural areas may be prohibitively expensive in others. Nevertheless, it might be possible to use such a scale to compare the performance of different options in a wide range of conditions and hence to establish where each may be effectively employed.

Timing

This substantial programme, drawing together the various interests concerned, tackling the development of ways of selecting different kinds of scheme for different approaches, and incorporating a full 'before' survey together with careful monitoring of the schemes set up, is naturally taking much longer than simply setting up an unconventional transport scheme in a particular area. This is unavoidable.

Two of the experiments were started by August 1977 while others started within a few weeks.

It will then be necessary to consider what advice can be issued quickly on the basis of the introductory work and subsequent stages as they arise, so that the lessons of the programme do not have to wait in the way that publication of research results so often drags on because of the need that is felt to get final conclusions precisely right.

Conclusion

In many areas the conventional bus is still the most suitable means of meeting rural transport needs. Elsewhere, however, it may not be able on its own to offer adequate services at an acceptable subsidy level. This is where unconventional services come in, but our knowledge of these is sadly deficient. We know from Norfolk that a village bus service driven by volunteers with public service vehicle licences can be established, break even and survive for at least one year. We also know that WRVS social car schemes can survive for a number of years without a very heavy subsidy. Post bus services have also proved very successful in a large number of rural areas. But in none of these cases do we as yet have any established methods for defining the sort of areas in which such initiatives could be expected to be successful or how they can best be integrated with existing services. Nor do we have any experience at all, naturally, of schemes which cannot be operated under the present licensing system. It is this additional range of knowledge and this experience which our experiments are set up to provide.

References

11.1 The Passenger Vehicles (Experimental Areas) Act 1977
11.2 Transport Policy White Paper 1977, Cmnd 6836

PART FOUR DISCUSSION
New Rural Transport Techniques
Chairman: Brigadier D.N. Locke

E.P. HINKLEY (West Sussex County Council)

When Mr. Glassborow was slightly critical of local authorities presumably he was referring to elected members. There are many county surveyors and planning officers and even some county treasurers supporting National Bus Company subsidiaries in what they are trying to do.

Mr. Glassborow mentioned that revenue/cost ratios in NBC's eyes are good, in the region of 90%, and the amount of subsidy was relatively low in consequence. Warwickshire undertook a study with Midland Red on the lines Cheshire are now attempting and found that bridging that 10% gap was extremely difficult for the reasons Mr. Glassborow indicated. Once services are reduced, associated revenue is also lost and reductions in overheads must be looked for. Thus, in order to approach a break-even situation, the services tend to be decimated. Mr. Glassborow indicated that the minimum standards being suggested by local authorities are too low. Why are they too low and what ought they to be?

P. WARMAN (Martin and Voorhees Associates)

The role of a number of people in the transport business has been discussed, including independent bus operators, transport coordinating officers, passengers, planning officers, etc. and yet no mention has been made of the role of drivers. If experiments are to be tried and evaluated in rural areas, this warrants particular attention.

For instance, talking to the drivers of post buses, it is interesting to note the increase in job satisfaction they feel from becoming better acquainted with the people to whom they deliver the letters in the rural areas. From research in West Yorkshire, there was found to be greater affinity between bus drivers and passengers in the rural areas than in urban areas. This was enhanced by the change to one-man operation. However, there is a tendency to have large rotas for drivers. This can mean a driver does not return to the same service for a number of weeks which does not encourage the relationship between drivers and passengers in the rural areas. There are often good scheduling reasons for this which try to maximize the use of staff, reducing 'dead' time at depots etc. but in rural areas this can lose the opportunity for the driver to supply the operator with valuable information on passenger travel habits and improve the friendly image of the service to regular passengers. The marketing role of the driver should not be overlooked in rural areas. Comparisons can be made with the taxi driver and the way he generates business in rural areas.

The driver, as the front man in the public transport business, is seldom discussed in his role for developing rural transport and yet, because labour is the biggest single item of cost and because of the importance of job satisfaction, marketing etc., the role of the driver could be a more prominent feature of rural transport experimental research.

R. BARRETT (Freeman Fox & Associates)

Mr. Milefanti noted that the experiments are designed to find out more information. Is not Mr. Glassborow's judgement being made before full evidence and full results are available to enable judgement on good and bad solutions in rural transport; what does he see as a solution to the rural transport problem?

D.W. GLASSBOROW (National Bus Company)

Many councillors are very helpful and very enlightened about transport problems. Nevertheless, minimum standards were probably too low. In our society there are two modes of life, the mode of life of those with cars and the mode of life of those without cars. Those people without cars tend to be very much deprived in certain areas. Mobility provided by a bus once a week on market day is simply not good enough. By linking town and land use planning and transport planning, people without cars could be given the opportunity to locate themselves in the places where there are good, and assured to be continuing, public transport services.

In past years conductors were the salesmen of the bus services. The move to one-man operation has done harm in that direction. It was most unfortunate that a wages problem and a particular set of rules at the time forced operators to adopt one-man operation with all the disadvantages for passenger and time-keeping, which have become apparent.

To return to experiments: they only deal with the fringe of the problem. Do not let them divert us from the major problem that so many bus services are failing to cover their full allocated costs. It is much more efficient to concentrate first on ways of keeping these services going and then to ensure that the passenger flows arising from our land use planning are provided with good bus services. This process could be successful.

D.C. MILEFANTI (Department of Transport)

In the experiments which have been given the acronym RUTEX (Rural

Transport Experiments) the drivers will be mainly volunteers and taxi drivers. Clearly drivers are an important element in any kind of service whether it is experimental or orthodox.

DR. C.G. DE KOGEL (Joint Management Organization of Regional Bus Operators in the Netherlands)

There are minibuses in the Netherlands but the mini-driver with the mini-wage is needed.

With the reported success of the Norfolk village bus experiment why are there not more than two or three places in the United Kingdom practising the village bus when this has indeed worked successfully for nearly two years? The village bus is described as making excursions on Sundays and taking people to the theatre in the evenings. If this occurred in the Netherlands, the taxi drivers in the neighbourhood would consider this as unfair competition. Is that not a problem in the UK too?

D.M. HOLDING (Newcastle Polytechnic)

An example of the possibility of combining bus and mail operations is the study for the Welsh Council in parts of Merioneth. This examined whether it would be possible to provide some form of bus transport as part of the postal operation. It was decided for various reasons that this was not possible. What was not considered was how the post got in and out of Dolgellau in the first place. Prior to the Beeching closures, trains carried the post and they also carried the people. The railways closed, rail replacement buses came in and the Post Office laid on their own vans. So the railway closures in fact, led to fragmentation. Should we not be thinking about combining the two again and talking about the kind of inter-urban movement between small towns which must be fairly important to the Post Office and where, in many cases, the post and the bus operators are duplicating each other.

Secondly, Mr. Glassborow refers to the idea of a flexible route to deal with the problem of villages which lie just off the main road. To miss these villages out means the people have to walk, but equally to take every bus off the main road up to the village would deter the people who are making longer journeys. He mentioned proposals for flexible operation where by booking in advance or by telling the driver, the bus would go off the main road on a demand basis. Superficially, the idea seems a good one so why, in fact, does he think it would not work?

D.N. BRUCE (Crosville Motor Services Ltd.)

Crosville Motor Services has recently been deeply involved with officers of Cheshire County Council in steering the work of the project team on bus

181

networks. Adding briefly to the remarks Mr. Knight made in Part Three, the purposes of the study, which is very much in progress rather than complete are: (i) To provide indications of the effects at different levels of future revenue support but not to provide planned network options for such different levels of revenue support; the distinction is important. (ii) To provide a starting point for town catchment area studies which in method may be similar to the Midland Red/Buchanan studies.

These will hopefully lead to soundly based improvements, adjustments and, where real savings can be made, reductions in the inter-linked networks of the urban, inter-urban and rural services. These studies will be linked in with the Structure Planning which Cheshire is engaged on, to provide the continuing basis for networks in the 1980s.

Where perhaps Cheshire differs at present from, for example, Oxfordshire is not only in its objective of supporting all justifiable bus services but also in its awareness that change does not come overnight and that the county has a responsibility to finance the often expensive transitional period.

As Mr. Keen suggested, subsidy need not lead to lethargy. In the past 15 months, Crosville has received something over three million pounds in subsidies. Per bus it received more revenue support than any other National Bus Company subsidiary. It has also implemented savings and revisions that have saved over one million pounds. This has not been achieved through lethargy.

D.W. GLASSBOROW

Dr. de Kogel asked about the Norfolk village bus experiment. Certainly it has done the job that was expected of it pretty well. On the latest figures it is breaking even, after allowing for some contribution to the original setting-up costs of the exercise. The Norfolk services are rather special. They were the first and it was a combined Norfolk County Council and NBC exercise, which may be the reason why they have not been widely copied. There were certain pre-requisites for it to work. There had to be enough volunteer drivers for those who were running it to be able to be sure that there would be a replacement driver available if one fell out. It was important that safety standards were not reduced by having volunteers and that is the case in Norfolk. They are qualified to drive these vehicles and they have all obtained their Public Service Vehicle licences. It is a success, but the test must come when some of the drivers dop out and others have to be brought in. Another important factor is that the man who is running the service, organizing it on a volunteer basis, is a real enthusiast. It will only work if someone makes it a particular hobby. On taxi competition, there did not appear to be any opposition from the local taxi man.

Mr. Holding suggests the combination of buses and mail carrying on a much more extensive basis—for some of the main movements of mail, and not just in outlying areas. There has been quite a history of buses carrying mail, but a problem is the security of the mail, particularly when vehicles break down and there are the difficulties associated with meeting Post Office timings as well as bus service timings.

On route diversion services, I referred to the desk study which was presented at the recent TRRL (Transport and Road Research Laboratory) Conference at Crowthorne on Unconventional Bus Services. The discussion there showed that there were potential problems. It is very discouraging to bus passengers, particularly at intermediate stops if you cannot tell them in advance that their bus has been diverted to a village and in consequence, they will have to wait another ten minutes in the rain.

P. DEAVIN (Norfolk County Council)

To make a success of a concept like the Norfolk bus needs the right kind of place and the right kind of people. It requires between 600 and 1000 people within a 10 mile (16 km) radius but sparsely dispersed. Herein lies the case for replacing scheduled buses by some other kind of service. The bus company asked Norfolk County Council to join them in the project. After some argument in committee the council found the money. Two of the villages already had their own entirely voluntary community car service. The old folk did not like that because they considered it charity. Charity from the rates was acceptable but not from friends.

D.C. MILEFANTI

The regular services of the Norfolk Village Bus appear to be running at a loss, but it is breaking even overall because of the excursions; also the excursions have attracted people who own cars. The bus has brought the villages together, so seems to be having a very useful social effect as well as being of specific transport value.

DR. R.J. BALCOMBE (Transport and Road Research Laboratory)

We were asked why we did not have more of these community buses in this country. The answer is that we do—there is one in Clwyd and one in East Sussex, both of which seem to be operating at least as successfully as the Norfolk one. We are hoping to set up another one in Devon as part of the RUTEX programme and it is hoped this too will be successful. It will serve an area with a rather larger population than that served by the Norfolk Community Bus, but this is perhaps one of the critical factors that RUTEX is designed to examine. If the area is too small, there just are not enough people riding on the bus to support it and it is hard to find enough volunteers to organize and drive it. The

183

opinion has been expressed that the population of the Norfolk area (some 600) is very close to the minimum for successful operation.

So what can be done in these marginal cases and places with even smaller populations? The answer here may be to revert back to a scheme using cars, not quite in the way described by Mr. Deavin, but in a new way under the legislation mentioned by Mr. Milefanti. Such a service can be available to anyone just like any other public transport service and you can allow people to pay fares to take away all connotations of charity. A properly organized scheme of this kind could be successful in the right place; the Rural Transport Experiments will eventually show whether or not this is right.

There have, in fact, been two fairly detailed case studies of diverting stage buses, the other being in Dorset where the implications were perhaps that it had a better chance of success than the Cumbria case referred to, but two case studies are insufficient to assess the general practicality of this concept. Although there are one or two private operators in various parts of the country who are operating on this principle, there has been no systematic examination of the resulting benefits or operating problems. One cannot at this stage endorse the principle as a general solution to rural transport problems, or write it off; one would need to see the results of a properly conducted experiment before reaching a judgement.

N.J. WILLIAMS (Greater Glasgow Passenger Transport Executive)

Subsidies have been discussed as though they were something new, but in fact it is a very old system which commenced in the cities and spread to the towns. Subsidies were initially introduced under the heading of 'reduction of hardship'. They were politically motivated and had the effect of retaining fares at a false low level. Had the fares been maintained at a correct level then, subsidies would not have been required, efficient operators would have remained viable, the recent heavy fare increases would not have been required, and many of the present problems affecting the industry would not have arisen.

Comment was made about the Traffic Commissioners and a desire expressed to disband them and transfer the work to the local elected representatives. Certainly the Traffic Commissioners are not perfect, but at least they are an independent body and do not make decisions with thoughts towards forthcoming local elections, etc.

The point of assessing need, rather than demand, is very important. The need of public transport is continually being increased by the centralization of other services, i.e. schools, hospitals, shopping areas etc. This situation is being created by planners and elected representatives, but in most cases, the bus operator is not considered in the initial discussions and this seems to be a failing. Bus operators should be involved at an early stage of any discussion to centralize a particular amenity, or any plans which affect the movement of people.

The provision of services to cater for *need* may not be viable and as such a subsidy may be required, and while objections may be raised to the bus company receiving a subsidy, is it the company or the passenger who is being subsidized?

Some areas have appointed transport coordinators and it is their initial job to ensure that best use is made of available resources. The coordinator is the link between all the interested parties and cooperation, not conflict, is an important part of this organization if an efficient public transport network is to be achieved.

We have heard about systems for the future, but the problems exist now and if we fail to solve the present problems, the planning for the future will be of little or no avail.

A.J. BOULT (West Wiltshire District Council)

There has been much discussion from people connected with the transport industry but little contribution from planners. It seems that probably the best the planner can do is to try and concentrate growth along the inter-urban bus routes because those are the ones that have got the best chance of not being discontinued. This pre-supposes that there will be growth in the rural areas along those urban routes. With the recent decline in population projection levels, (in West Wiltshire there has been about a 6% population growth per year over the past 10 years) the signs are that there is ample scope for the reduced growth to be accommodated in the town limits without sprawling out into villages and making them commuter centres. Perhaps it would be too naive a question to ask the local bus company the minimum size of settlement for which they could provide a direct bus link to the nearest town.

There seems to be some evidence that it is cheaper to move goods rather than people. If this is so, then perhaps on minimum costs there is a good case to create more work places in villages, a point made previously by Professor Wibberley. Perhaps this would increase the prosperity to the extent that they would buy more cars. What would happen then to the public transport from that village? If, as planners, we try to encourage more employment in rural settlements, are we going to be accused by the transport people of being anti-public transport?

B. DELVES (Pembury Parish Council)

I represent the person much maligned in the discussion, being a parish councillor, a do-gooder and a member of a pressure group! I represent the user rather than the operator of rural transport. In the discussions there has been insufficient emphasis put on the planning aspect.

I come from the village of Pembury in West Kent with a population of

185

approximately 6,500 which has grown from about 2,500 over the last 17 years. In that time two shops have disappeared and there are no additional facilities whatsoever. There are over 600 houses that have no car or even recourse to using someone else's car and there are problems with the National Bus Company. Special concessionary fares for old age pensioners do not exist and children pay full fares at peak periods, something like 16p to travel rather less than 2 miles (3 km). The biggest problem is the bottleneck situation where about 90 children have to be conveyed to one particular school in about half an hour, but by setting up our own unconventional bus service, this will hopefully be overcome.

D.W. GLASSBOROW

Mr. Williams talked about the false low level of fares and how they have now risen, which is worrying.

Something is known of the short-term effect of the recent fares increases but nothing at all is known about the effect they are going to have in the long term. One thing which causes concern is the pressure a county council can exert to force the operator to seek fare increases as a means of reducing revenue support. With reduced subsidy the operator has the dilemma of fare increases or reducing services. Generally, because people matter, the operator against his better judgement will increase the fares. This process may cause considerable difficulty in future years.

If as an individual, you can be sure that that village between two towns is assured a reasonable bus service, you may well move there of your own accord—you don't have to be planned to go there. The problem of declining population growth is a difficult one for planners as it is for everyone else. At one time planners talked about the relocation of non-conforming uses. What about in a more general sense the relocation of non-conforming people who want bus services but will insist on going to live somewhere where they cannot have one. If people can be assured that for the next ten to fifteen years there will be a good bus service for a particular village, that gives them the opportunity to decide to move there.

D.C. MILEFANTI

Regarding Mr. Delves' problem with school children, we know this is because of the peculiar form of the legislation on statutory transport of children to school. Successive Secretaries of State for Education and Science have tried to tackle this, but oddly enough the parents, who are at the moment having completely free transport for their children to school, do not seem to see it in anything like the same light as those who are having to pay the full fare and this so far seems to have prevented any rationalization of the situation.

186

DR. M. HARRISON (West Yorkshire Passenger Transport Executive)

In 1971 the NBC following a financially difficult year, effected significant service reductions in certain rural areas. In West Sussex, the villages of East and South Harting and Nyewood, having lost their hourly services to Midhurst, Chichester and Petersfield were left with only irregular services and in consequence, the villagers decided to raise funds for a community mini-bus. During 1975, that bus was operated on a schedule which was circulated through the villages and the schedule was such that the minibus preceded certain of the remaining Southdown stage carriage services by about 20 minutes to and from Petersfield. As the stage carriage service is a route serving other communities, both east and west of Midhurst, and of necessity a double-deck bus route to cope with the peak movements to the very large secondary schools in Midhurst, one must surely question whether that is the correct way for the community bus service to be operated. It is essential that the objective should be clear and the effect understood before such services are introduced.

K. HOLMES (Hertfordshire County Council)

The structure plans and local plans are prepared by the county and district authorities. The policies on transportation and in respect of public transport are laid down in the structure plans and, theoretically at least, they are supposed to be translated at the local level in the district plans or the local plans. Planners, operators and public transport coordination officers must be brought into working discussions for both structure plans and local plans. Planners should recognize when they are producing their district plans that public transport has a very important role to play. All transport coordinators should be taking full account of this. They should ensure that policies on public transport are brought in to the local and district plans.

J.E. WRATHALL (Huddersfield Polytechnic)

Several contributors have commented on the need to remember the user of rural transport services, but no-one has attempted to define the consumer. Even Mr. Milefanti in listing the people involved in his Central Steering Committee and in the local area groups did not list the plain ordinary person with no axe to grind. Perhaps consumer research is needed to ascertain the ways in which different groups assess the demand or the needs of the rural dweller for transport services. What methods are being used to assess and monitor the transport requirements of the rural dweller on a continuous basis?

D.C. MILEFANTI

The Harting community bus mentioned by Dr. Harrison is a special case

187

because of the way in which it is operated which, apparently side-steps the licensing system by simply running a raffle. The other community buses described have all been through the licensing system which means they have had to justify their case before the Traffic Commissioners. This is a very important point for future development in this kind of field.

It is very difficult to get the views of ordinary people. In the case of the rural transport experiments, the first stage was to get as near to the ordinary people as one could. The working groups had on them representatives of the parish councils as a whole in the areas, Women's Institutes, Women's Royal Voluntary Service, etc. These are all people very close to the ordinary people who live in the villages. Furthermore, Dr. Balcombe in carrying out his preliminary assessment, wrote to large numbers of individual Women's Institutes and other bodies in individual villages. The only way to get closer to the people is by a household survey to find what the individual households really want. This can be done in the case of experiments and this will be done in the rural transport experiments before any of the actual services are started. However, such a survey is very expensive.

D.W. GLASSBOROW

Mr. Holmes is right when he suggests that operators and planners should talk to each other far more and talk at the early stages when plans are being prepared. They must learn each other's language, because planners' jargon and busmen's jargon can often lead to misunderstanding.

Regarding consumer research, the NBC are trying to develop a continuous study of passenger needs, following initial work on assessing what passengers did before and after fares increases in about ten different locations in the country. In time a more continuous understanding of the factors which effect travel in those particular areas is hoped for.

J. WICKS (Martin and Voorhees Associates)

It has been mentioned a number of times that consumer research is difficult, costly and cannot be justified. Of course, certain types of conventional survey are all of those things, but consumer research has a wide repertoire and embraces a variety of techniques which can be adapted to suit particular situations. For example, the study I am involved in at the moment, West Yorkshire Transportation Studies, has been working on a policy for rural transport within the county of West Yorkshire and incorporated a programme of social research involving the use of psychological investigation. The method adopted was that of the semi-structured interview and within the rural areas of West Yorkshire just over 600 interviews were carried out—not an excessive number considering the size of that county. The approach does need particular expertise and each interview is quite lengthy, but the actual number of interviews, the cost of the research and the time taken was minimized because it did not require massive sampling procedures, questionaire printing, computer analysis, etc. There are many different types of consumer research appropriate to particular situations and needs and too narrow a view of the subject should be avoided.

D.W. GLASSBOROW

It is important to know whether these methods give the answer at an acceptable cost. On one occasion a study of this kind was planned. The firm concerned were so disappointed with the result they did not even send in the bill. The results from such studies are surely very doubtful.

CHAPTER TWELVE

Conclusions

R.J. Balcombe

Looking back on eleven chapters and the discussions, the problem of identifying and developing the more significant themes and conclusions is compounded by a dominant impression of discord: different groups of participants put forward opposing and, in some cases, extreme views, and there is little progress towards common ground. This no doubt reflects the realities of public transport and transport policy, in which institutional and organizational problems often overshadow those of planning and operating services. These issues are import- ant and open discussion of them is to be welcomed if it promotes mutual understanding and possibly consequential benefits; nevertheless, they must be related to the basic objectives of country planning and how it depends on and in turn affects rural transport.

Two major questions seem to have remained unanswered: 'What kind of rural society are we trying to maintain' and, 'What is the nature of the rural transport problem which we need to overcome?' It is recognized that rural communities are changing—the proportion of people employed locally (mainly in agriculture) is declining in favour of those who commute (mostly by car) to urban centres, and the retired—but there are no convincing arguments for trying to stem the tide: just a vague dislike of change. In any case, there seems to be little that planners can do about it. The encouragement of local industries to provide job opportunities for the young might help, although it is not in itself sufficient, especially in the context of increasing centralization of retail, educational, medical and other facilities.

Transport, especially public transport, seems to come remarkably low in the country planner's list of priorities. There are perhaps two basic reasons for this. The first is the great disparity in time scale between planning, whose full effects may take decades to materialize, and transport which can respond rapidly to changing demands. However, there is real concern among transport operators that there should be at least medium-term stability in their financial resources in order to allow efficient management, and among planners who have to speculate on the quality of public transport services in the fairly distant future. The second point is that public transport is very much a minority mode in rural areas, and therefore has little impact on planning for the majority.

Perhaps the essence of the rural transport problem is that facilities are adapted to (if not planned for) the needs of a mobile, car owning majority; the carless minority is too small and too widely dispersed to provide worthwhile loads for conventional bus services. There are three basic options: to provide no public transport; to subsidize a basic level of transport along conventional lines; and to try unconventional means of catering for low levels of demand. The first option is generally considered unthinkable, except perhaps in areas which have never been served by public transport, and where the residents are presumed to have adapted to their circumstances and to be in no need of help (although the validity of this view has yet to be tested systematically). If services are to be provided and subsidized there is general agreement that they should be designed to ensure maximum value for money or, more often in a period of economic restraint, a basic level of service at minimum cost, although it seems impossible to reach agreement on what the basic level should be, or who should determine it. It is generally, but not universally, held that local authorities, who have the overall responsibility of coordinating and, where necessary, supporting, public transport, are best placed to assess local needs and determine what services should be provided. But there are extreme minority views: on the one hand local communities (rather than counties who are too remote to be sufficiently sensitive) should assess their own transport needs and propose solutions, subject only to the general guidance and overall financial control of local government; on the other, standards of service should be set nationally, to prevent irresponsible authorities from ignoring, and failing to provide for, the universal needs of rural people. The first of these approaches was criticized on the grounds that it implied abdication by local authorities of their responsibilities for coordination, and the encouragement of an inefficient, piecemeal pattern of service. The second approach seems, on close examination, to contain an inconsistency: while its objective is to provide for everybody's supposedly equal needs, the level of service proposed depends on the'population of the community served and individual needs are not equally met. The implication is that standards must be modified locally to match available resources, and that local government is better placed than central government to ensure that this is done sensitively and efficiently.

Setting levels of service, which is fundamentally a matter of balancing realistically assessed local demands against what can be provided at a reasonable cost, is only part of the much wider and more complex function of coordinating public transport. Coordination of services requires coordination of several bodies—the various tiers and departments of local authorities and other public bodies and operators of all kinds working together as teams to produce structure plans and Transport Policies and Programmes which can be properly executed. Ideally, the traffic commissioners should be seen as members of such teams, rather than as referees between opposing sides. It is perhaps still too soon to judge how well the new arrangements resulting from local government reorganization, as well as the implications of the Transport Policy White Paper, are working; some of the complaints voiced in this book may be due to teething troubles rather than fundamental weaknesses.

It is clear that coordinated transport networks in rural areas will continue, as long as they are maintained, to consist mainly of conventional bus services (although the future role of the railways in rural transport is doubtful). But they will not be static: there must be continual monitoring and adjustment to the changing needs of society; operators and local authorities must be willing to experiment with new routes and timetables as a means of assessing demand. However, the conventional bus service is not the optimum solution to transport problems everywhere: it is already disappearing in more remote parts of the country, and there are places it has never reached. While car ownership is (of necessity) high in such areas, and lift-giving is common, there is concern about the difficulties, and possibly hardship, experienced by a small minority who have no car or cannot drive and must rely on neighbours for help. The studies being conducted as part of the programme of Rural Transport Experiments (RUTEX) will help to determine the extent and degree of the problems of this minority, but the programme will do more than that: it will make practical tests of possible new solutions. There is as yet no clear dividing line between the areas best served by different forms of transport, and it is unlikely that RUTEX will define one: a more realistic objective is to demonstrate how all kinds of transport, both conventional and unconventional, can be coordinated into effective and economic networks.

Index

193

Southdown Motor Services Ltd. 40
Stage Carriage Services 15, 46, 97, 98,
　　101, 108, 113, 114, 125, 131, 132,
　　165
Strathclyde 31, 32, 155, 156, 172
Structure Plans 8–15, 35, 47, 56, 57, 86,
　　94, 114, 116, 127, 147, 182
subsidies 9, 10, 11, 21, 33, 34, 37, 40, 46,
　　50, 51, 57, 62, 66, 70, 81, 90, 94, 95,
　　97, 98, 101, 128, 130, 133, 135, 162,
　　184
Surrey 101
surveys 40
Swansea 154
Sweden 134-136
Switzerland 135, 154, 156

taxis 125, 167, 170, 180, 182
Tiverton 172, 174
Tollesbury 140
tourism 124
Town & Country Planning Act (1971) 8
Trade Unions 101, 151, 171
Traffic Commissioners 31, 58, 98,
　　100–102, 114, 126, 132, 153, 166,
　　170, 184, 188
traffic congestion 9, 10, 15, 95
traffic growth 108
trams 19
Transport Act (1962) 161
Transport Act (1968) 69, 127–129, 132,
　　139, 140, 143, 161, 166
Transport, Department of 53, 76, 86, 91,
　　96, 109, 116, 146, 170, 172, 176
Transport Holding Company 161
Transport Policies & Programmes 62, 74,
　　75, 78, 80, 85–89, 107–118, 125,
　　127, 147, 192
Transport Policy White Paper (1977) 8,
　　46, 62, 70, 125, 146, 170, 192

Transport and Road Research
　　Laboratory (TRRL) 165, 170, 183
Transport Supplementary Grant 8, 11,
　　47, 52, 55, 74, 76, 83, 86, 91, 92, 94,
　　96, 109, 110, 111, 114, 116, 128,
　　147
Transport Users Consultative Committee
　　(TUCC) 153, 170

Umberleight 174
United States of America 69, 146
Utrecht 17, 19, 29, 30

vehicles (cost of) 63, 65, 163, 165
villages 4, 12, 13, 35, 37, 38, 48, 53, 56, 57,
　　59, 62, 65, 99, 102, 115, 123, 124,
　　155, 162, 168, 181, 185, 186

wage costs 10, 131, 137, 163
waiting times 136
Wales 150, 155
Warrington 69, 112
Warwickshire 179
Welsh Council 150, 181
Welsh Office 170
West Suffolk Report (1971) 47, 49
West Sussex 93, 187 ——
West Yorkshire 39, 40, 179, 188
White, P.R. 57, 58
Wisbech 139
Women's Royal Voluntary Service
　　(WRVS) 125, 170, 177
work buses 46, 65
work hours 39, 49, 136
work journeys 14

York 74, 89

Zeal Monachorum 174